'I NEED to write a boc

'I have a book inside

Two cries I've hearc
graduates and clients. Now
resource for them.

What Karen has created here is magnificent. Why? Because not only does she TELL you how to structure, write a book, publish it, fit it into your whole business model. Not only is it beautifully written, easy to read, packed with information, step-by-step instructions and utter wisdom.

No, more than that.

What Karen does in this book is to SHOW you and TELL you at the same time.

The book models brilliantly the exact process she is teaching. She demonstrates as she teaches you.

Why is this so fabulous?

Because, as you read this book, you're receiving its message on two levels. Your conscious mind reads the information, and says logically to itself, "Hmm, that makes good sense!"

All the while your unconscious mind is taken gently by the hand to play in the sandpit of creativity, where it quietly watches as Karen artfully installs and inspires you to take action. The result is you'll find yourself up at 5.30am writing "just a few more lines" before you even get to have your morning cup of tea.

It's subtle, effective and clever. Very, very clever.

If you have a book stuck inside you, no need for surgery. Read this and your book will just slide out onto the page and into the world and published.
– **Dr. Lisa Turner**, Psycademy and author of *Spiritual Guide to Riches* and other books

An excellent, no-nonsense and comprehensive guide to writing and marketing a book. With clarity & wisdom Karen Williams cuts through all the 'blah blah' about publishing and tells you precisely what you need to know. Affirming, practical – a great read.
– **Sarah Lloyd-Hughes**, Ginger Training & Coaching and author of *How to be Brilliant at Public Speaking* (Pearson)

Finally, an easy to read and well-structured resource that helps you create a book that is designed to grow your business. Writing a book is one thing, but structuring, designing, publishing and marketing a book so that it builds your brand and brings in new clients is a whole different matter. I particularly loved the chapters on how to self-publish and put together a marketing campaign to promote it. I wish this book was around when I published my first book; it would have saved me making the basic, newbie errors that I am now avoiding with my second.
– **Karen Skidmore**, Speaker and Marketing Mentor and author of *Shiny Shiny*

Karen Williams is a star! *Your Book is the Hook* covers the step-by-step process of writing THE book which will elevate your profile, your credibility and your business to exciting new heights. Imagine you're at the bottom of the success staircase.

Karen climbs every step with you – until you're jumping around together at the top, where your dream clients can clearly see you and REALLY want to be with you! This is your plan; one which brings together your wildly creative, notes-and-thoughts-all-over-the-place into a structure which will serve you, your business and your clients in incredibly fruitful ways. It has inspired me to reach more clients than ever before and create new and unique content. *Your Book is the Hook* combats overwhelm, brings in organisation, pushing your business and message into alignment and out to the world!
– **Lyndsey Whiteside**, Starmaker and PR Expert

Karen Williams has done it again! *Your Book is the Hook* is full of inspiring and practical advice and guidance on how to plan, write and publish your book so that it aligns with your business, helps you stand out from the crowd, gives you credibility and brings you more business. Karen holds nothing back. Using her experience as an established author with an Amazon bestseller, Karen shares how to get your book out of your head and published in a step-by-step easy to follow guide. *Your Book is the Hook* has given me the skill and confidence to plan and publish my first book!
– **Emma Heptonstall**, Coach and Legal Expert, Divorce Alchemy

I loved this book! There's a wealth of practical 'how to' exercises and resources together with many inspiring case studies. I have been procrastinating about my book and now realise what a dis-service I am doing to the women I work and connect with! The book is packed with tips, ideas and

proven strategies. I loved the last few chapters. A must read if you are serious about growing your business!
– **Sandra Green**, Women's Leadership Coach, Handbags in the Boardroom

Your Book is the Hook is full of practical steps and contains everything that you need to start – and most importantly, actually finish – writing your book. In addition, Karen includes some incisive questions to challenge your thinking on what will be the most appropriate book to write to reflect your business. Karen writes as an accessible, honest and supportive friend offering many tips that she has tried and tested, reflecting her integrity. Highly recommended!
– **Rachel Bamber**, Leadership Coach, Brighter Thinking

Karen packs a lot of content and insight throughout her book and programme. It's inspiring to learn from someone who's been there, done that and really is walking her talk!
– **Gill Davis**, Leadership Coach, Kincavel Coaching

Before I started working with Karen, I had loads of ideas on many bits of paper but that's all they were. Within a week, the tips Karen provided unlocked something and I couldn't stop writing; be warned you may find yourself writing through the night too! The programme really focused my attention on my business and I now have a very clear vision for the future.
– **Sally Betts**, Digital Learning Consultant, Ideas4learning

I'd been planning a book for some time and Karen's system was exactly what I needed to get my thoughts and ideas into a workable form. Most helpful for me was the guidance on tailoring our book to our ideal client. This unlocked my creativity and allowed the ideas to flow. A book is a major undertaking and Karen's support has been invaluable in keeping me focused on my goal. With her quick-thinking yet kindly approach, Karen was a marvel at helping me to pull my ideas into shape. I recommend the book, programme and Karen highly.

– **Tina Radziszewicz**, UKCP Registered Psychotherapist

I have been thinking of writing a book for a few years now as I have developed my niche but somehow didn't link that with the content of the book. Karen has expertly supported me in focusing my thoughts and the needs of my target market so that it is easy now to organise all those haphazard thoughts, into chapters and books. I've gone from overwhelm to focus. Thanks Karen!

– **Vicki Raven**, Well Kids Mentor

Your Book is the Hook

How to Write, Publish and Promote the Book that will Build your Business

To Caroline,
With best wishes on your book journey!

Karen
x

Karen Williams

ISBN 978-1-849146-24-1

Typeset by Shore Books, Blackborough End,
King's Lynn, Norfolk PE32 1SF

Contents

Foreword

Writing a book is one of the best ways to establish yourself as an expert and thought leader, and if you've picked up this book to get noticed in your industry, you won't be disappointed.

We first noticed Karen when she published her first book. Before then she'd been under our radar, and it certainly helped her to become visible and grow her business. Tim attended the launch party of her first book in 2011, and we've known her ever since.

As published authors ourselves, we know the impact that writing a book can have on your business, and we're delighted that Karen has now published her third.

We also know that it's not just about publishing your book; it's about having the other systems, products and marketing in place to support it. This is where Karen has got it right. As well as supporting her clients to write their books, she helps them to put the infrastructure in place to ensure they align their book to their business, and use it to raise their credibility.

In this book, Karen has simplified the process that makes it easy for coaches, consultants and therapists to write their best book to reach more of the right clients. It's a process that we wished we'd had years ago, because, like Karen, we've made our own mistakes. Also there are other books that teach you to write a book, but not many tell you why, or what to do alongside it, that enables you to monetise your knowledge.

If you've decided that it's your time to step up, you've made the great first step by getting a copy of Karen's book. Now it's your turn to make it happen. Your book is the hook that will help you to reach more clients and grow your business, and in her book, Karen teaches you the six steps to achieve this easily. We love Karen's style of writing, which gives you a great structure and logical steps to follow, that will make writing your book a realistic and rewarding achievement.

We are delighted to be supporting Karen with this book and her business, and we know that reading this book – and implementing the strategies, of course – will make a huge difference to yours.

Emma Sargent and Tim Fearon
The Extraordinary Coaching Company

Acknowledgements

Your Book is the Hook was never intended to be my third book. I actually had another one on the go, which ironically then went on the back burner.

This book came about by default when I realised that I had an effective writing, publishing and marketing process to share with my clients, and developed a programme to do so. It wasn't long before I decided to turn this knowledge into this book. Having written four books over the last five years, and having helped many of my clients to do the same, it was the perfect next step.

I couldn't have written this book without the coaches and consultants who joined me on this pilot programme during the summer of 2014, the ladies who joined me in Spain for the first writing retreat, and my clients who I'm supporting on their business and book journeys.

It's great to have a support team looking out for me too, including my brilliant VA, Tracy Harris, as well as everyone who has helped me to make this book happen, and Emma Paxton who has been responsible for the brilliant images that accompany this book. I'd also like to thank those who have contributed their time and words to the case studies and expert tips that will inspire you.

I'd like to acknowledge my family and husband who motivate and support me. I want to especially thank my Dad for continuing to inspire and drive me, despite not being here anymore. I couldn't do this without feeling your pride and approval deep inside, and I miss you picking up on my grammatical errors!

Lastly, I'd like to acknowledge you for taking the time to read this book, and I'd also like to recognise your commitment in advance for taking the actions that I suggest. I would love to hear about your journey with your own book, how I can help you, and I look forward to continuing to inspire you to stand out.

You can contact me via my website, follow me on Twitter or like my Facebook page:
www.selfdiscoverycoaching.co.uk
www.twitter.com/selfdiscovery
www.facebook.com/selfdiscoverycoaching

You can also access additional resources and bonuses related to this book at:
www.yourbookisthehook.com/downloads

Chapter 1
Why you need to write a book

You may be thinking that anyone who wants to be someone is currently writing a book. It seems like it's the "in thing" to do, and it sometimes feels that everyone is talking about it. But that's because it works! When you want to grow your business, reach more clients, and increase your income, your book is the hook that will do this for you.

Now here's the thing: Your book won't make you money. It's not going to be your retirement plan. Actually you're probably going to spend weeks if not months agonising over it, wondering if you're doing the right thing, and worrying about whether you're ever going to finish it. You're going to be trying to fit it in around other priorities and sometimes you'll be wondering if it's worth it.

You will probably feel anxious about getting your stuff out there. You may start to doubt yourself, wonder if you're good enough and who is going to read what you have to say – let alone like it!

But you are here for a reason and there must be something that has triggered you to want to write your book and be reading this page.

I'm sure that you can see the importance of writing your book, leveraging your expertise and building your credibility. I'm sure that you also know that getting it right first time, learning some of the shortcuts, and making the most of this opportunity, will help you too.

You may also be thinking how good it will feel when you have finally written your book, where it allows you to make a bigger difference, reach more people and do more of what you love in your business. It will give you the confidence to do things that you've never dreamed of approaching before, and give you access to opportunities that you'd love to make happen.

Let me remind you why you're here and what you'll get from writing, publishing and marketing your book!

Why your business needs a book

As I've already mentioned, your book probably won't make you a millionaire. Very few people reach these dizzy heights, and if this is the reason why you want to write a book, then it isn't for you. But if you see the potential that your book will give your business, then I want to give you some examples of how it will help you. I hope that this will keep you motivated as you take the steps to create your own book through the process I'll be teaching you, and keep you on the straight and narrow when you wonder if it's worth it – because it is!

When I refer to writing a book here, I'm talking about a non-fiction book that will support and grow your business. With increasing competition for services, being an author will give you the credibility that sets you aside from others in your profession. It will open doors that have remained shut before. Imagine you want to attract new business where you have no contacts already. Will a letter and a flyer make a difference? Or would your book get you an appointment more easily? It makes a huge difference when you have this tangible product that allows you to demonstrate your knowledge and credibility.

It is brilliant tool for your marketing, allowing you to attract more leads, as you demonstrate what you know already in a physical form. This will help you to get more speaking engagements, publicity, and attract new business more easily than you can with just a website, blog and a handful of business cards. When you introduce yourself as a published author you'll be recognised as someone who knows what they are talking about and as an expert in your field.

When you align your business to your book – which I'll be teaching you here – it will help you to create multiple product streams from your knowledge and expertise, thus giving you new ways that people can buy into your know-how. This will help you to reach more people and ultimately enable you to make more money than you can from your one-to-one time.

By strategically using your book, you will attract other people who want to partner with you and refer clients to you, and it will increase your presence in your industry and profession. Quite frankly, I'm sure that you can see that your brilliant book is better than a letter, a brochure, a tweet or a sales call!

This book is for you if you are a coach, consultant, therapist or trainer who understands the importance of what you know already. You've made the decision that you want to stand out from the crowd, are ready to make a bigger impact, and that you're in business for the long haul. You want to reach more people, make a difference, and your book will allow you to do this.

What makes this book different from other books on writing and publishing?

There's plenty of advice available to help you to write your book. But achieving success in this area is not just about writing any old book, it's about writing a great one that supports your business, and creating a business that supports your book. That's what makes this book different from any other information you'll find on writing and publishing.

Actually writing your book doesn't really start until around halfway through *Your Book is the Hook*, because you've got to nail your business first and put an effective plan in place to make it happen. Then you can sit down at your computer and bring your masterpiece together and get it published.

You'll also find out how you can leverage your expertise. You'll learn how to make the most of the knowledge you have – the things that you find really easy – and discover how to teach this in a way that allows you to make a bigger impact with your clients.

Plus I'll share with you the secrets to use your book as an effective marketing tool and get it in front of the right people, use it to grow your business, and strategies to make the most of what you know – your intellectual property.

And if that's not enough, you'll learn from my experiences of writing four books. I'll share my mistakes, what I've learnt and dispel some of the myths and mysteries that will allow you to make the most from your words!

I will teach you the six stage process that I follow to write my books. I'll also share stories to show how other people have used their books to grow their businesses, and the successes that they have achieved through getting their knowledge onto paper.

Why I have written this book

Before I move on, let me introduce myself properly and tell you why I have written this book. I'm Karen Williams, a business coach and book mentor, and I set up my business, Self Discovery Coaching, in November 2006. You can read my full biography at the end of this book, but in summary, I struggled during the early years of being in business, and I noticed that many coaches and other business owners were also achieving mediocre success.

It was due to this observation that, as part of my Neuro-Linguistic Programming (NLP) Master Practitioner course in 2009, I decided to model the mindset behind a successful coaching business. I initially interviewed 11 successful coaches, who were not only great in their profession, but successful in business too. I learnt their secrets and their strategies and applied them to my own business – and they worked – and it wasn't long before I realised that I was learning information that other people needed to know too. This research became my first book.

The Secrets of Successful Coaches was published in 2011, which became an Amazon bestseller. I went on to interview 13 more successful coaches as part of my launch plan. During this process, I identified what worked and developed my own Seven Step Success System, which I started to teach to coaches and therapists in business. I share this strategy in my second book, *How to Stand Out in your Business*. Both of my books have allowed me to reach more people by becoming a respected published author, and they have enabled me to grow my business and reach greater successes.

As well as writing and publishing this book, my next book, *The Mouse that Roared*, is also coming soon, and I have also contributed to four other publications. This is why I have modelled my own experience and the work I carry out with my clients to give you the information I know and help you to write the book that is your hook to grow your business.

How to use this book to get started

Before I launch into the first section, let me tell you more about *Your Book is the Hook*, what to expect, and how to approach it.

For your book to be successful, we'll be focusing on your business first. Unless your business is book ready, then writing a book will be a total waste of time. You need to know where you are an expert, and how you can package up your knowledge.

You also need to get to know your prospective clients and readers before you put pen to paper. You need to find out what they want from you, and how your book will help them. You'll focus on what's already been written in your area of expertise, and what makes you and your book different.

It's only then that you'll get started with your book. But before you document a single word, you'll create your best book by planning first. I've come across plenty of writers who stare at a blank screen, start their book and never finish it, and I'll give you the strategies and shortcuts to write your book quickly and easily.

Once you've done this, it's time to start writing, and bring all of your knowledge together into a neat package that allows you to use it as a business tool. You'll be learning how to make your book stand out so that it reaches more people, builds a community of people who love what you do, and gets you noticed.

Of course, I'm sure that one of the things that you want to do is get your book published, and I've done the hard work so you don't have to! I'll help you to navigate the publishing maze, and give you some great resources to help you to get your book into the hands of the people who want it.

Then lastly, the most important part is marketing your book. In the final section, I'll give you strategies to get to the top spot on Amazon, get your book noticed, and use your book to grow your business.

This is the type of book that you'll probably want to read from cover to cover at the start. This means that you can get a full overview of the structure that works and what you need to do when you write your book. I also see you dipping into sections more deeply when you approach certain areas, like when you are getting your book published, and specifically when you are ready to market your book.

As well as my strategies, I've also asked other experts to share their snippets of advice to give you additional insights on topics related to writing and promoting your book. You'll also be inspired by stories and case studies from my own experiences and other people who want to motivate you to get started by sharing some of their personal results.

In each chapter you'll also find a review of the most important points so that you can easily see the next steps, as well as access the other resources available from my website that supplement the information in this book. This includes a pictorial blueprint of each section, which will help you to see how each part fits together. If you can't wait to get instant access to all of these bonuses, please go to my website now and register at www.yourbookisthehook.com/downloads. Are you ready to get going with your book? Let's get started!

Section 1
Are you book ready?

Many books have been written about writing, publishing and marketing books, but very few focus on getting you and your business book ready.

Creating a book-ready business is about putting the infrastructure in place first to make the most from writing your book. Is it really worth spending your time on this, if you don't have the systems, processes and clients in place to get the most from your book? This is where many authors fail; they don't have the right structure to use their book as the hook to grow their business and attract more clients.

When I talk about you and your business being book ready, I mean that you:

• Are crystal clear about what you want to get known for and why you are the expert in this field. As well as developing a wider reach, you'll also want to use this book to build your credibility, expert status, and be ready to stand out and tell people what you think and believe in.

- Are totally clear on your ideal client and what they want from you. You will probably be working with this group of people already, and know what their problems are and how you can help them. You may even have a signature system that you've developed, which teaches what you do in a step-by-step fashion.

- Will have a product funnel in place which serves your clients, allowing them to tap into your knowledge and expertise in different ways. You'll probably have a lead magnet or ethical bribe (aka your freebie) on your website, where prospects exchange their contact details for a report, e-Book, video series or MP3 programme that solves one of their problems. You may also have an information product (or more) that is aligned to your business, or be considering developing it. Plus you'll probably be running events and offering one-to-one services where clients can work with you on a bespoke basis.

- Already have a community of people who love what you do, and potential joint venture partners in complementary professions who will support you. You'll be connected with large numbers of people through social media, many of whom you've developed relationships with on a personal basis, plus people you know through your local networks.

- Will also know what else has been written about your subject and who your competitors are in this field. You'll know if you've identified a gap in the market or how your book is different from others who have already written material in your area.

- Will probably be known in your industry already, albeit you might not be the star of the show. You'll be talked about by your peers, be speaking at events, or getting press coverage in your area of expertise. Or, if you are not known already, you'll have contacts in this area, who will support you when you launch your book.

Don't worry if you haven't got all of these in place right now, as I'll be teaching you about these first before you start to think about your book!

Read on and let me show you how.

Chapter 2
Be an expert in your business

When I carried out the research for my first book, *The Secrets of Successful Coaches*, I was staggered by the statistics quoted to me. Apparently 10% of coaches are successful, and the average coach earns less than US$20,000 a year.

This data indicates that very few coaches achieve business success, which I certainly established whilst writing that book. I also know that this is similar in other professions where you're providing a service. Of course, success can mean different things to different people, which is one of the concepts I explored in that book. When I talk about success here, I mean those who are attracting most of the clients and making the most money in their industry.

In 1906, an Italian philosopher, Vilfredo Pareto, introduced the concept of the 80/20 rule. He observed that 80% of the land in Italy was owned by 20% of the population; that 20% of the pea pods in his garden contained 80% of the peas, and it wasn't long before this concept was applied to business and success. This would indicate that:

- 20% of business owners have 80% of the clients and income.
- 80% of your profits come from 20% of your customers.
- 80% of your sales come from 20% of your products.

- 80% of success is down to your mindset and 20% comes from your ability.
- 80% of your results come from 20% of your actions.
- 80% of businesses don't make it.

If we take the first couple of points, you need to be in the top 20% of people within your profession. These are the ones who are most successful, attract the most clients, and get the best results.

If you don't feel like you are in this percentage at the moment, you probably don't yet stand out from everyone else.

This is what most people do when they don't stand out. They create a similar website to their competitors, they have a similar message, and then (not surprisingly) they get similar results. They struggle to get noticed, they find it hard to attract clients, and then they give up and go back to their day job – the thing that they wanted to get away from in the first place.

The other problem is that many people don't do enough of the right things to become visible. They think it's enough to set up a website and hope. I remember being told by one of my mentors once that hope is not a strategy! You have to be proactive, get yourself 'out there' and tell people why you are the best person to help them.

If you are serious about standing out, then you need to be able to demonstrate your expertise. If you are serious about your business, then one of the best ways to do this is to write a great book –

and I believe that this fits into the 20% that you should be doing! But if you want to write a book, you need to be an authority and demonstrate your expertise. Not only will this help you in your business – by being different from everyone else in your industry – it is a great positioning tool and a way to get you noticed.

Get clear on your niche

If being an expert is a step too far right now, the first action to take, before moving forward, is to define your niche. I'm sure that you know this already: if you write a book that is aimed towards appealing to everyone in the population, you'll struggle to be successful. It will also prevent you from writing a book that establishes you as an expert in your field. You want to have a particular group of people in mind when you are writing your book, and it makes sense that you choose the group of people whom you are working with already.

In my first book, I talked extensively about niching. However, things have moved on over the last few years. These days, you don't have to choose a 'traditional' niche. When I qualified as a coach, it was implied that we had to become a 'health coach', 'career coach', 'redundancy coach' or suchlike, when I actually believe that you can have any niche you like as long as people want it and will pay for your services! Actually, choosing something unusual is more likely to help you to get noticed.

However, it is still true that there are two main types of niching.

The first is where you niche narrow and deep. An example would be a hypnotherapist focusing on helping women with stress, or a coach working with professionals on money management. Although it could be said that both of these niches could be a little tighter, it would be relatively easy to get known for doing each of these things.

The second is where you work with a specific group of people. In my business, my niche for the last few years has been working with solopreneurs (predominantly coaches, therapists and other service-based business owners) and helping them to put marketing systems and client attraction processes in place to stand out in their business.

Or you could take it one step further, like I have in this book and in my business now – you could call this a micro-niche. I still work with coaches and therapists, but I've chosen to specialise in one particular area to help this group to stand out, i.e. by writing their book; however, the business side of things is still vitally important.

Why you need to be an expert

Niching is just the first step, and then you need to learn to stand out and be an expert. A great model that will help to explain this is the 'Pyramid of Power and Profit' originally penned by Dan Kennedy. This takes niching one step further and it will demonstrate why niching isn't enough by itself!

In his research, Dan identified four levels of

expertise and this is my interpretation of the model.

Generalist – this is the bottom level of the pyramid. Most people in business are generalists. Using the coaching example, if you are a generalist, you will be a life coach. You will be offering your services to anyone and helping them with anything. You'll be trying to be all things to all people, but will not have an obvious specialism, let alone a clear idea of your ideal client. Ultimately, you will struggle to achieve success. The main problem is that your offering will be fluffy, indescribable and no one will understand what you really do. In a nutshell, you won't have a niche!

Specialist – when you have decided to niche, this is where you are initially likely to be. You will have a specialism and can communicate this to people. They will have more of an understanding of what you do and the results you give your clients. This is where you have decided your niche, and will be helping a certain group of people with a particular problem to find a solution in this area. I also think that there could be an additional level next, as a true specialist for those who niche deeply. For example, you may be an EFT (Emotional Freedom Technique) practitioner focusing on helping new mothers to cope with postnatal depression, or a coach who has chosen to specialise in working with musicians to help them with their career or business.

Expert – this is the next section in the pyramid and people generally reach this level when they have written a book or are known for what they do, hence the importance of this section in my book. They are recognised as an expert or go-to person in a particular field and do something that makes them stand out from the crowd. With regards to the pyramid, I'm sure that you can see how there are fewer people in each level as you move up towards the top (remember that 20% that I mentioned earlier?).

Celebrity – this is the top level. Examples of people in this area are Paul McKenna, Anthony Robbins, Michael Neill; people who are perceived as celebrities in their field and are regularly in the media, charge high fees, and can sell out venues.

Where are you in this pyramid?

Where do you want to be?

What makes you an expert?

If you want to become an expert, how are you going to get there?

In Malcolm Gladwell's book *Outliers*, he stated that it takes 10,000 hours of practice to become an expert in something. So if you want to be an expert and never eat, sleep or do anything else, it would take you 417 days to become proficient.

How does that sound? Wow, really, so what is an expert?

If you search online, the first definition that comes up is this: "Having a great deal of knowledge or skill in a particular area". Does this mean that you have to immerse yourself for 10,000 hours first? Well I believe not.

That's not to say that the advice given above isn't important. I don't advocate promoting yourself in an area where you don't have any experience, but I also believe that being an expert is more than immersing yourself in a particular specialism.

We all have knowledge and experience that will benefit our clients. I believe that I have credibility in the area of helping coaches and therapists to stand out from everyone else in their profession – and I also know a thing or two about writing a book! Throughout this book I've modelled what I've done in terms of growing my business and writing my own books, and I'm helping you to do the same.

Although in saying this, I generally find that it is easier to acknowledge your failings than to celebrate what you are good at, and many of my clients struggle to define where they excel. This is likely to be because this is what comes naturally to them, so it isn't an effort to do this thing. Actually that thing that you find easy is probably what your clients need to know.

If you're struggling with this right now, then you need to nail this area first before you start to write your book, so let me give you something to try out.

In my second book, *How to Stand Out in your Business*, I shared what I call the 'Passions and talents exercise'. Here it is, so take some time to do it now.

Passions and talents exercise

Take a couple of pieces of A4 paper and give yourself around 15-30 minutes to do this exercise thoroughly.

On the first piece of paper, write the word 'Passions' on the top of the page. Then take some time to write down your passions.

What do you love to do? These are the things that will get you out of bed in the morning or the things that you'd do even if you weren't paid for them.

On the second piece of paper, write the word 'Talents' at the top of the page. Then I'd like you to write down your talents.

What are you good at naturally? These are the things that you do naturally without thinking and may not even recognise as talents because they seem easy to you.

Put both pieces of paper in front of you. Then I would like you to ask yourself this question: "How do they fit together?"

Free bonus: you can download this action sheet for free at my website:
www.yourbookisthehook.com/downloads.

Even if you already know where you excel, you might find this exercise useful. There may be additional areas that you haven't considered before, or perhaps you are not yet expressing where you really shine!

Another exercise that may help you in this area is to carry out a SWOT analysis and this is where you look at your strengths, weaknesses, opportunities and threats, usually in conjunction with a goal you have set yourself. Let's take writing a book for example; you could easily do a SWOT analysis on this topic to see where you excel and where you need support. This may help you to make decisions about what you do yourself and which parts of the book process you need to outsource. You can also access more information on this topic at www.yourbookisthehook.com/downloads.

There are many advantages to being an expert. Or if you don't like that word, think about it as demonstrating your credibility or being in a place to share your knowledge and experience.

Going back to my comments earlier about what makes you an expert, I believe it means that:

- You don't have to know everything, but I would expect that you are many steps ahead of your clients. You'll be known for what you do and add value to the clients that you have already.

- You'll have extensive knowledge and skill in that area, and be able to share this with your clients. You'll probably have plenty of stories and experiences to share. You may also be taking steps to increase your learning and always be developing your expertise.

- People get what you do and your message is clear. People have certain expectations when they hear from you and when they employ you to help them. Your reputation will precede you and you'll be known as the go-to person in this area.

- You'll position yourself in a certain way to attract a specific group of clients, and you may also be charging premium rates for your services.

- You'll also be clear about what you want to get known for and be projecting this to your clients.

- You'll probably also have contacts who can support you and your clients in particular areas. For example, in this book I've asked other experts to contribute as I respect their knowledge and how they can help you too.

If you're not yet convinced about why you need to be an expert, then let me share Marianne's story.

Case study: Marianne Page, author of *Process to Profit*

Writing a book is first and foremost a great way of convincing you how good you are, and giving you real clarity around the mountain of value you have to offer.

Out in the marketplace, it will establish you as an authority, give you ownership of your ideas, and it will pitch to your ideal clients for you, so that they come to you pre-sold, fully understanding what you have to offer and how you can help them. "I read your book on holiday, and realised I need your help," was how one client put it.

Since my book was published, I've increased my turnover by 300%. And clients, who previously I would have had to work very hard to attract, have come to me... That's the beauty of a book!

Marianne Page
www.bright7.co.uk

What do you want to get known for?

Success is not just about being an expert; it's about doing something you love too. So I ask you: What do you want to get known for?

This is one of my favourite questions, and one that I ask all of my clients. Once you are really clear on your response, it will change your business. But it's also a very difficult question to answer. I should know, as I remember a time when one of my clients turned the tables on me and asked me what I wanted to get known for!

The first thing that most people will say in response to this is often a little fluffy. These are things like "I want to get known as a brilliant coach", "I want to get results" or "I want to help people". None of these really say what you actually do, or the results you provide, do they?

To rephrase this question, I could ask: "In which area would you like to be the go-to person?" This would help your contacts to understand what you do and say to their friends, "Go and see 'insert your name', he/she is the go-to person for 'insert expertise'."

You'll probably be leading the way in this field; perhaps you are a thought leader or are working towards this label.

 Top tip: One way to approach this is to consider how you would like someone to introduce you at a networking event. What would you like them to say about you? Sure it would be nice for them to say that you're a brilliant coach, hypnotherapist or nutritionist, or that you get results, but what do you really do?

I'm sure that you can see why it's not enough to be just another coach, therapist, etc, and it may take you a little while to dig deep to get your own answer. The most successful entrepreneurs, especially within the service-based professions, are totally clear on exactly what they do and why they are the best person to do this.

When I spend time with my clients on a one-to-one basis, this is something that we take time to nail together, because it is often something that is difficult to recognise. It's also a question that I'll ask many times during our sessions together as it may develop over time.

Let me give you an example:

I remember a particular VIP day I ran for a couple of clients, both of whom were new coaches. When I asked the question "What you want to get known for?", initially the response was a little vague, but by the end of the session I got a stronger response. One of the ladies said, "I help people to get more from their money". Although this is work in progress, isn't this clearer than "I want to be a great coach"?

But don't worry if you're a bit vague about this right now, or you're not sure exactly what you do, as it will come in time and may also develop alongside your book.

Before I move on, let me recap the most important part of this chapter. Before you even think about writing a book, you need to know where you excel and where you are an expert. This is the first step to creating your book-ready business.

Things to think about

Get clear on where you are now in terms of being an expert.

Also make sure you know where you want to be in the pyramid, why it's important to you, and how you are going to get there.

If I were to ask you, "What do you want to get known for?", what would you say?

If you're still struggling to see where you are an expert, list five reasons why your clients should come to you over any of your competitors.

Chapter 3
Get to know your reader

Being clear on what you want to get known for is great, but when it comes to creating a book-ready business, you've also got to know who needs this message. In this chapter, I'd like to give you some advice and ideas on how you can do this.

Who is your ideal client and reader?

Have you ever identified who you really want to attract in your business? It's important that this person is not only someone you can help, but someone you would love to work with as well! Getting clear on this ideal client or reader that you are targeting will enable you to understand what they want from you. This will help you to write your book.

When I'm working one-to-one with my clients, this is one of the areas I ensure they focus on right at the beginning of our relationship. Knowing the type of person you want to appeal to is essential before you start to do any marketing – but I often see people who leave this important part until much later! This is usually when they find that what they've done already isn't getting them any enquiries or leads. This is when many people realise that they are a generalist and that their strategy doesn't work.

Let's start by defining who it is that you want to

work with in your business. There are a couple of ways in which you can do this. I'll often ask my clients to come up with an avatar (or picture) of their ideal client, where they identify the following:

- Their gender

- Their age

- Their profession and earnings (and socio-economic status)

- Family life and children

- What they do and where they hang out

I'll also ask my clients to give this person a name and perhaps a picture too. When you are always focusing on this one particular person, it will help with your marketing, communication and your message also.

If I think about some of my clients, their avatars are very different from each other, even though many of them are coaches and therapists. For example, if you want to appeal to a jobbing musician, your language and website copy will be very different from one where you are aiming to communicate with the Human Resources (HR) Director of an educational establishment. When you know who you want to work with, it makes it easier for you (and your book).

 Top tip: It is really important that you identify your ideal reader and write to this one person in your book.

What are your reader's problems?

When you want to find out more about your ideal client, it's not just about identifying who they are, you also need to find out:

- Where is that potential client in their life right now?

- What's going on for them?

- What are their problems, struggles or challenges?

When identifying this, I've been known to draw a stick person in the middle of a piece of A1-sized (flipchart) paper and ask my clients some of the following questions:

- What is this client frustrated about?

- What are they moaning about when they're with their colleagues around the water cooler/ having coffee with friends/out for a drink with their mates?

- What are they worrying about when they wake up at 5am and can't go back to sleep?

- What are their biggest fears?

- What stops them (from making the change or difference that you can help them to make)?

These are great questions to identify your client's problems and pain, as knowing these will make it easier to plan and develop your book, and you will be able to delve deeply into the best areas to focus on when you start to write it.

Another way of identifying your client's problems is to simply identify who in your network fits into this category and ask them! Here are a couple of ways you could do this:

You could offer to take this person out for coffee, lunch or dinner, and let them know that you want to ask them some questions about your business and your book.

Or you could do a survey and ask people to respond to carefully worded questions that help you to identify your ideal client's challenges and what they want instead. This may be a short question in an email to your community, or a survey using a combination of qualitative and quantitative questions to get their feedback on specific areas.

When I was creating this book, I ran a Summer Book-Camp – three webinars which were delivered live throughout August 2014. This not only allowed me to promote a six module programme that I'll mention later, but it also enabled me to find out what questions my clients had when it came to writing and publishing a book, many of which I've addressed in this book!

To stand out from the crowd and create a book that is the right hook for your business, it needs to solve your client's most pressing problems, and give them a solution that works.

What does your reader want from your book?

You've taken the time to identify your client's problems, so what do they want instead? Your book needs to consider where your client is now, what they want instead, and then help them to bridge the gap.

It is important in this area to be as specific as possible. For example, saying things like "feel better", "live a better life", or "reach their dreams" just isn't going to cut it, I'm afraid. This is fluffy like the example I gave in the last chapter.

Of course, asking your clients what they want and using their language is the best way to do it. As a professional yourself, you may find that you use jargon from your training, rather than the actual words that your clients use every day – and it's the latter which is essential. When you've identified what you think your clients might want, go deeper and ask yourself...

- What will that give them?

- Which means that...?

These questions are great, because they go beyond the features of what you offer and delve into the benefits, solutions and outcomes that your client wants.

Imagine that you have a client who is stressed at work. Through having a conversation with her you identify that she keeps getting passed over for promotion, and she feels that her boss is thwarting her progress. She also feels that she is doing much of the work of this position anyway, but is not getting rewarded for it financially, nor is she getting any thanks. She is starting to feel victimised and wondering what she has to do to get noticed.

This client may have approached you because she has got to the end of her tether, and wants to get a job elsewhere where she is respected and supported. It is your job then to help her get clear on what she really wants.

If you are coaching her, you will probably help her to look at her problem in more detail and seek a variety of solutions. For this lady, the grass may not be greener on the other side, so you may consider how she can approach her boss in the right way. You may also help her to get clear on her transferrable skills, to excel in an interview situation, to cope with the effects of the stress, and more.

Do you see what I mean about being specific?

That's why it's important to dig deeply into this area. It's very easy to focus on what you do, when ultimately your prospective client wants to know what it is going to give them – the benefit. Ultimately people don't buy coaching, acupuncture, counselling, etc, they buy the result that they are going to get when they work with you.

Although you'll probably find that every client is different, I'm sure that there will be themes that you follow when you work with people in your area of expertise.

How to nail your wow factor

The way you approach your clients and your message will be the thing that gives you the wow factor, which leaves your prospect feeling understood. Let me give you some examples.

- When you've spoken at a networking event and delivered your introduction or elevator pitch, and you hear a chorus of 'oohs', or you have a line of people who can't wait to speak with you.

- When you have a client contact you because they've read your website or other marketing copy, and they feel like you are speaking directly to them.

- When you've written the book that addresses the needs of your ideal client, which means that they are now clamouring to connect with you, and engage your services to support them.

Do you see where I'm going with this?!

Although you may have decided where you are an expert, going deeper into this process allows you to really put yourself in your clients' shoes. Just think... If you had a problem with your teenagers, wouldn't you want to see someone who specialises in working with someone exactly like you – and had published a book that was entitled *How to cope with your teenagers*?

If you wanted to write a book, would you go to a general business coach or would you go to someone who has written and published books, and achieved success in this area?

I rest my case!

The clearer you are on your ideal client and where you are an expert – and why – the easier it will be to write your book.

Develop your important message

Lastly, in this chapter, getting clear on your ideal client and reader will also help you to focus on your topic, and how to approach this area. It will also help you to understand how you can bring all of your knowledge together into something that people want to read.

For example, my overarching message in this book is to inspire you to write a book that will help you to get noticed. I want to give you a structured process to making this book easier to write, publish and promote. What do you want your book to do for your readers?

Developing your message will also help you to develop your book-ready business in more detail, and I'll be covering this next.

Things to think about

What do you need to do now to get clearer on your reader (and ideal client)?

Who do you know who can help you?

What do you need to do to nail your wow factor?

What problem(s) do you need to solve in your book and what message do you want to project to your readers?

When you download your free resources at www.yourbookisthehook.com/downloads you'll also get access to a special discount code to get access to my membership club (www.thebusinesswowfactor.com). If you want to create the wow factor in your business, this is jam-packed full of inspiring interviews and actionable blueprints.

Chapter 4
Develop your
book-ready business

Once you've nailed where you're an expert, your niche, and your ideal client and reader, it makes it easier to develop a business that is book ready. To remind you what this means, this is what happens when your business and your book is aligned, when you have clear next steps for your clients once they have read your book, and when you use it to leverage your knowledge and expertise.

In this chapter, I'll be helping you to take the next steps to get your business book ready. You may have some of this in place already, which is great, or you may need some additional support to get focused. Although if this is the latter, don't worry too much, as you can develop some of this alongside writing your book. I'll be giving you some examples as I take you through the next steps.

How to create a signature system or process

In the summer of 2011, I worked with a mentor to develop my signature system. I already knew the thing that I did well, and what I wanted to get known for. At that stage in my business, I was working primarily with new coaches and therapists in business who wanted support with its development, marketing and growth. I had found that there were particular processes that I typically covered with my clients, plus activities and advice that I shared. But I didn't have a system. At the time, I wanted to get clear about what I really did. She helped me to create a signature system based on this and it completely changed my business.

When you have a signature system in place it helps you to get known for what you do, as you have a structure to follow and people see the process that you use. My signature system is the Seven Step Success System (based around the acronym SUCCESS). This is what I did to showcase this system and reach more people:

- I decided to write a book about it! This was my second book, *How to Stand Out in your Business*.

- To help me to write the book and give me some deadlines, I ran a programme at the same time where I taught the concepts to a group of clients. This meant that I could check the system worked, get immediate feedback and add huge value too. As a bonus, I got paid for it at the same time. This programme later morphed into '90 Days to Stand Out in your Business' which I delivered very successfully in 2013, and is the backbone to my membership club – www.thebusinesswowfactor.com.

- I was able to develop the material and test it with real people as I wrote the book. I was also able to ask questions and make sure that the important elements were included.

- I developed an e-Course where I shared the main principles, which later became part of my lead magnet in 2013.

- I recorded a professional video which outlined these principles, and shared this through YouTube and on my website.

- I was able to share what worked with clients who got results through following the seven steps.

- This is the process that I generally teach one-to-one with my clients now, and is pretty much the steps that you need to follow to create a book-ready business!

The process for *Your Book is the Hook* is actually one of the sub-steps of my Seven Step Success System. When I started to put this book together, I developed the process by modelling what I've done myself and what I teach my clients already. As I wrote this book, I did so alongside delivering a six module programme (of the same name). It certainly motivated me to write it in a very timely manner!

I also help my clients to develop their own systems based on their knowledge and expertise, as it gives them a process to follow with their clients. It also helps them to articulate what they do well, to document the steps on paper, and see where they excel.

 Top tip: Once you've developed your system, give it a name so that you have a memorable process to share with your clients.

Your process or signature system will help you to write your book. It will give you a clear structure to follow, and you'll be able to break your knowledge into manageable chunks. This will also help you to get clear on what to include and what not to include in your book. This is particularly important if your goal with your book is to give people a taste of what you do, and how you do it, before they decide to work with you.

Steps to build your list and product funnel

When I engage a client who wants to stand out in their business, after nailing their niche and ideal client (and perhaps creating a signature system), I work with them to find people who love what they do, build their list and create their product or sales funnel.

Those business owners who are in the 80% of people getting just 20% of the clients are often those who mainly offer one-to-one services to their clients, and to be in the top 20%, you need to have a funnel in place.

This simply means that you have to have multiple products and services available to your prospects, and these will usually lead logically into each other.

You'll often start by having something free in place at the top, otherwise known as a lead magnet (or ethical bribe). This will be available on your website and offered in return for someone's name and email address. As long as you are providing something that your clients want, you'll start to build your list.

If you're not sure what to give away as your freebie, here are a few examples from some of my clients:

- A sleep and relaxation MP3 recording, which accompanies the work of a hypnotherapist who specialises in helping people with stress and anxiety.

- A three part video series, which supports the work of a healer and trauma coach.

- A seven part e-Course for female Sales and Marketing Executives, where the coach teaches her seven step Clarity signature system that I helped her to develop for this audience.

Get clear on the biggest problem faced by your clients and solve this in your freebie. It's certainly not enough these days to advertise something like 'Sign up to my newsletter' on your website as people are much more discerning when it comes to giving their personal details, because excessive emails can lead to overwhelm. But offering something of value (this needs to be your best stuff, by the way) will encourage subscribers, especially if the title is intriguing, it addresses a problem, or creates curiosity. I remember one such lead magnet that I used to have on my website was called '20 reasons why you can't make money as a life coach'! Not surprisingly, it was quite popular.

Then you need to keep in touch with your subscribers regularly. By using a newsletter provider (like AWeber, Mailchimp, or Infusionsoft), you can set up a series of autoresponders that are automatically sent once someone has subscribed to your list. You will also send regular broadcasts or newsletters to keep in touch with your community and build a relationship with them. You'll be sharing great content, and interspersed with this information you may also share promotions relevant to your business (and your book, of course!).

In your product funnel, you will next have a pathway for your subscribers. The next step is likely to be a low-cost product, which may actually be your book once you've written it. You may offer this directly when your new subscriber signs up for your free offering.

Then you may have an information product (or two). This could be an online programme, a membership club (like The Business Wow Factor – a continuity programme with ongoing monthly membership), or an event or workshop. With all of these ideas you are providing a one-to-many approach rather than a one-to-one service. You're also selling more than your one-to-one time, hence resulting in a potentially higher profit when you get it right.

At the bottom of this funnel, you'll have your one-to-one packages, VIP services or mastermind programmes available. This is where you work with clients in a bespoke way, although you may be using your signature system to help them to get the results that they desire.

What you will find, however, is that some people will be ready to work with you on a one-to-one basis without experiencing each of these levels, and actually your book will help you them to bypass these. Your book will enable you to have informed conversations, and attract clients who feel that they know you and the way you work through reading your book. They understand what you offer, how you can help them, and they are more likely to want to work with you personally.

As I mentioned earlier, don't worry too much if you don't have all of these in place right now, but be prepared to develop them as you create your book. The advantage of having a community of people who love what you do is that it is the perfect place to tell people about your book, and create interest before you even finish it!

How to build your online and offline presence

Another way of building your community is through your online presence. Often my clients ask me whether they should be on Facebook, Twitter, LinkedIn, YouTube or any of the hundreds of other platforms available. Your online presence will help you to build your book-ready business, however, trying to be on all of the social media platforms all of the time may not help you to get your book done! Working out where your clients are is essential, and creating your online profile now will help you to market your book.

When people start to get to know you and what you do (and where you are an expert!), this will build your credibility and you will start to get noticed. My biggest piece of advice in this area, however, is to make sure you build your own list at the same time. Although social media has really helped me to grow my business, you never know when platforms like Facebook will change the goal posts, and you could lose your online community forever.

When you know what you want to get known for, it makes it easier to get noticed online. You can share tips related to your expertise, you can write blog posts that showcase your knowledge, and you can use the online world as a platform to share advice or strategies that might work for your community. I'll go into this in more detail in the final section on marketing.

Developing your offline or physical presence is also important. Whether you attend networking events, go to larger conferences or become a speaker (a great way to stand out), this will help you to get noticed, as well as helping you to build your network. When you are launching your book, having joint venture partners who will support you is equally as important as potential clients. This will help you to reach more people than you can do alone.

I do attribute much of my success to my connections, and a combination of online and offline approaches work for me. For my clients, I can refer them to other people who are complementary to me for additional support outside of my expertise, and I will share other people's advice later in this book as well.

Put essential systems into place

Lastly, in developing your book-ready business, you have to put systems into place. If you are going to be truly effective as an expert, you need to run an efficient business. This means that you will outsource tasks that other people can do better than you, and ensure that you take action to support your business growth.

Your book will propel you into a different place, and having your systems in place now will help you later on – I promise. This might include a series of autoresponders that go out to new mailing list subscribers as I mentioned earlier. It might also be a tried and tested process when you launch a new product or when you run an event. It might be a plan in place that allows you to easily write regular blog posts and then share them with your ideal readers. You may also want to get help now from a business mentor to get additional support, advice and accountability, and a virtual assistant or PA to support you in the areas where you need it.

Things to think about

Get clear on the processes that you tend to follow with your clients and start to create your signature system.

Consider the products and services that your clients want and how you can provide them.

Focus on other ways to get noticed that will also build your business and develop your book.

Look at the systems that you need to have in place that will support your business growth, and the people who you need to help you.

Action points to create your book-ready business

Who is your ideal reader?

What book do they want?

What problem does it solve?

What book are you actually going to write?

What is your hook?

If you're the type of person who likes to visually see information in a mind-map format that takes you through the different areas in this section, you'll want to go to my website now to download the blueprint for this section and all of the bonuses: www.yourbookisthehook.com/downloads.

Section 2
What makes your book different?

One of my clients recently asked me: "Do I really know enough to add to the millions of books already out there?!"

When you are writing a book, your task isn't to regurgitate everything else that has already been published or produced on your topic, your job is to create something unique and different. For example, you may well see similar information elsewhere – as this isn't rocket science and other books have been published on this topic – but here you get my experience and my angle on the subject.

Before you even think about your hook or your unique angle, the next thing you need to do – after getting clear on your niche, ideal reader and what you want to get known for – is this: what you are actually writing about in your book? I gave you a few questions to think about at the end of the last section. Did you do this? If so, what were your answers?

I also hope that you've developed a clear reason why you are writing your book, as this will keep you going when the going gets tough, when you start to doubt yourself or you wonder if your writing actually makes any sense! When you know what it will give you and your clients, it will make it easier to stay motivated, to get finished as well as started, and to get your message out to the people who need it. I'll be sharing some strategies here that have helped me to get my message out through my books.

With this in mind, are you ready to get clear on your content and what makes it different?

Chapter 5
Getting clear on your topic

When you really understand your ideal client and what they want to know, it makes it easier to write your book. Your subject matter will become more defined, you'll be able to go narrow and deep into the topic, and your readers will be ready to devour your knowledge and expertise.

I believe that having a niched book is important when you are writing an expert book, as you'll want to use this medium to demonstrate your expertise. If you want to be recognised as a thought leader, visionary or influencer, this is a brilliant way to do it.

In the first section, I asked you to consider the systems and processes that you teach your clients, and this would be a very good starting point. As well as identifying the problems of your clients, your book needs to be written within an area where you have extensive knowledge. I also believe this should be an area that you are passionate about as well. For example, I teach my clients to stand out and become more visible in their business, and there are various ways to do this. They can get speaking engagements, attract great PR, get noticed on social media, to name but a few. But my passion is writing, and I also know the difference it has made to my business. It makes more sense for me to share this expertise with you, and there are other people who prefer to focus on different ways to stand out.

How to get clear on your book topic

If you're anything like most budding authors, you've probably got lots of ideas and it may take a little while to nail exactly what is most important to you and your reader. So if this is your first book, let me ask you some questions.

- What book do you need to write that will set you aside from other people in your profession?

- In what area of expertise do you want to get noticed?

- What do you want to get known for? (Yes that old chestnut again!)

If you're not yet sure, get to know your potential ideal clients and what they want to know. I suggested this earlier and if you've already got a community of people who love what you do, why don't you simply ask them?

This will make it easier for you as you'll be creating a buzz already, you'll be answering their needs in your book, and you're more likely to know that you are writing about the right thing!

Take some time now to refine your topic further. Once you've decided what you are writing about, then you can go deeper into the next step.

- What do your readers really want to know?

- Why should they buy it?

- What will they get from reading it?

This is where working on the problems that your readers are facing will be useful for you, as you'll have an inkling of what to write rather than feel overwhelmed with all the information that you could share. By the way, even if you're writing great stuff, you need to know why people will buy your book, as not only will you need to write it, you'll have to promote it too! I'll be talking more about this later. Consider what your reader will get from the book, so that you make sure you cover all the bases in your writing.

At this stage you may find a few doubts going around in your head, and it's OK to be nervous. Here are two questions I've been asked previously and I thought this would be a great place to give you my answers.

One of the questions that I was asked was: "How do you know when to stop with respect to cramming too much information in the book?" When you are considering the information you want to provide, this is where structure and planning is important, which I'll be going into in more detail in the next section. Although the answer to this question will depend to some extent on what you are sharing, your book needs to have a structure that your readers can easily follow, rather than jumping around from point to point and confusing them. If you have lots of information to share, why not write two books?

You could say that I've done this. In my second book, *How to Stand Out in your Business*, I touched on the topic of book writing in one of the chapters and knew that I had plenty more information to share on this topic. I deliberately kept this section easily digestible. But in this book I have had the opportunity to go into much more detail.

Conversely, another question I was asked was: "How do I find enough information to go into a book?" This was a really great question, and this may well be going through your mind at the moment. You might be wondering if you know enough or whether you have sufficient knowledge to share, and if it helps, many people go through this thought process.

 Top tip: Start by making a note of everything you know – and I mean everything – and why this is important information that you need to share with your readers.

How to make it easy to write your book

Let me tell you a secret: your book doesn't have to be an encyclopaedia or hundreds of thousands of words in length. By the way, if you don't feel you have enough information to go into a book, here are a few suggestions to help you:

- Ask other people to contribute to your book, especially in areas where you feel their expertise is greater than yours. This may be entire chapters or sections where they can share their ideas with your reader. To show you how to do this, I've asked a few experts to contribute to this book.

- Share relevant stories that support the teaching in your book. I've done this in here as it shows you why you need to write the book and the results that others have had from doing this.

- Interview other people to get their opinion and include these thoughts in your book, attributing these to the individual. If you've read my first book, *The Secrets of Successful Coaches*, you'll see how I did this.

- Do some research to find out what other people think on the subject, for example via the internet or other publications. Although it is important to state here that you must not plagiarise other people's copyrighted work. (I'll be covering best practice and legalities later.)

- Carry out a survey or ask your clients what they think, like I did through the Summer Book-Camp that I mentioned earlier. This was a great chance for me to ask my community what they'd like to know about writing a book and answer them here.

- Pose some questions on Facebook or LinkedIn and find out what people think. This especially works when you do this in a group where many of your prospective clients hang out. Although be careful to acknowledge the rules of the group so that you don't alienate the administrator if it's not you.

It's important to note that 11,000 new business books are published each year in the US alone* (which doesn't take into account self-published books and e-Books). That means that you have to know what makes your book different, that you don't repeat information that is already in the public domain, and you've got to get clear on your hook. We'll be doing this next!

*Source: www.businessweek.com and Jack Covert, CEO of 800CEORead and *The 100 Best Business Books of All Time*.

Things to think about

Get clear on your topic before you start writing.

Go narrow and deep into one subject rather than trying to share too much information in one book.

Be prepared to do your research and develop your take on other information available.

Always have your ideal client in mind when you create the content for your book.

Chapter 6
What is your hook?

There is a reason why this book is called 'Your Book is the Hook'. This is because the focus is on helping you to write a book that is the hook for your business. This book will help you to stand out from everyone else in your profession, enabling you to grow your business, and is the platform to build your credibility in your area of expertise.

What else has been written on your topic?

The first thing to do – before you get clear on what makes your book different and your hook – is to understand your competitors and find what else has been written on your subject already.

If you've been in business a while, I do hope that you already know your competitors, in terms of other people in your profession who do something similar to you. I also hope that you know what makes you different to them.

Well the same applies to your book. Before you even start to plan or write your book, I suggest you check out books written in the genre or category of book that you are about to start writing.

There are a few ways of doing this. The simplest is to go onto Amazon or another online bookstore and search for your topic. You may choose to search in general or specific terms to find out what has been written. For example, when I searched the term 'Marketing', there were 145,849 results, but when I searched for 'Marketing for coaches' there were 1,012 results. This is still a sizable number, but if I wanted to write within this niche, I could check out the most popular books easily.

On Amazon, many books will offer the 'Look Inside!' feature where you can check out a sample of the book, including the chapter headings, introduction, and normally around 20 pages.

You could also go into your local bookstore, although many books that are published these days are only distributed online, so this may not give you an accurate competitor analysis. However, it will allow you to peruse the books on the shelf without needing to purchase every single book in your proposed topic area.

If you are writing a book in a specific niche and already have credibility, you may have many of these books on your bookshelf anyway. I know I have! I'm always intrigued about what other people have written on the topic, and their unique point of view.

How to find your angle or hook

I'm assuming that by now you have decided the topic for your book, even if it needs a little refinement. Also you'll have done research around the area of your book and have found out what other people are saying about this topic. The thing that will make your book different is your hook and unique angle on the topic. For example, when creating a book about writing and publishing, there are various different angles I could have taken.

- I could have focused it on one singular aspect of writing and publishing a book, like how to get published on Kindle, going even narrower and deeper than I've taken this book already.

- My angle could have been on how to use your book to grow your subscriber list and community.

- Or I could have focused explicitly on how you could use your book to make money in your business.

- Perhaps I could have written a book solely about how you can create a signature system to write your book.

Now these ideas came to me in just a few minutes, and perhaps there are a few more books here too! So with your topic, why don't you do the same?

My unique angle with this book is to show you how to align your book to your business. My focus is on how you can use it to build your credibility and demonstrate your expertise. I want you to apply these concepts to both your business and your book to truly stand out. Also my target readers are coaches, therapists and other business owners who can see the value that writing a great book can add to their business.

Your unique angle and hook will set you aside from other people in your industry. It will help you to grow your business if you follow the process that I've covered in this book. Just accept that the book itself won't be your retirement plan, but the resulting work will help you to build your business. I know that this process works!

When considering what makes your book different, just like in business, you are what makes your book unique. People buy people and I'm sure that you've found that some clients have started working with you because you've taken the time to get to know them and vice versa. Actually your book is a great way to help people to get to know, like and trust you too, which is an added bonus.

This means that you need to showcase you in your book. You might be sharing elements of your life and personality that you've never done before – and this can be a little bit scary. Even in this book, where I share practical steps, you'll get an insight into my experiences and what I've learnt from them. Especially in an expert book, your style and personality will make an impact on your readers.

The importance of sharing your story

In your book, you may wish to share stories, which will resonate with your readers. You may be writing your book because you've gone through something difficult yourself, and now you are ready to share your expertise to help others avoid your pain. This, of course, is one of the reasons for this book. Actually I was asked two questions about stories, so this feels like the ideal time to answer them.

One of the questions I was asked in the Summer Book-Camp was: "How do I make my story of value to the reader?" and the other was: "Is my story interesting enough to write a book on?" I believe that stories are incredibly powerful, and when you are willing to share your experiences, it will enhance your book.

There are many ways of doing this. You could seed in stories throughout your book to demonstrate various points, a little like I've done throughout this book. These don't have to be your stories, and may be those of your clients – just remember to seek permission and adhere to confidentiality – or other notable people if they are relevant to the information that you are sharing.

If you prefer, you could share your story as a whole book in itself (like an autobiography or your memoirs), which is used to demonstrate an important point like overcoming adversity. I've done this in *The Mouse that Roared*, which shares the story of my life, and how I went from a shy child to a successful entrepreneur, and some of my learning along the way.

To do this, it's helpful to follow the principles of the 'Hero's Journey' as outlined in Joseph Campbell's book by the same name. To give you a brief overview, you firstly share the 'old story' (which is where you used to be), then you build the story by telling the reader more about your struggles, the key moments (which may be vivid, fascinating and emotional), taking people on a journey to a climax of maximum intensity, ending with your closing message and what happens next. If you've watched any 'TED Talks', many of these speakers follow this process.

Top tip: Even if your book is not solely about you, getting clear on your story and why you're writing the book is still important, and I suggest you start to document your life story now. If nothing else, it is incredibly cathartic to get your thoughts down on paper, as well as what you have learnt from various things that have happened to you.

The final option would be to write a book in the form of a narrative following a character's journey. Books like *The Alchemist* by Paulo Coelho, and one of my favourite books of all time, *The Monk who Sold his Ferrari* by Robin S. Sharma. Let me give you a short overview of how this works in the latter book. The story goes as follows: the main character, Julian Mantle, reassesses his life after having a heart attack. He then sells his Ferrari and undertakes a spiritual journey to the Himalayas. The main part of the story is when he teaches what he has learnt to his friend John. The reader learns lessons through the narrative rather than through a step-by-step process. Both books actually follow the 'Hero's Journey' process if you look closely.

Stories will take your practical tips to the next level. They will also demonstrate what happens when you do or don't do something, and they will engage your readers in more ways than you can through words alone.

If you think about how stories have been used throughout the centuries, from generation to generation, they also help you to remember things, where sharing things on a practical level may not have the same effect. A story will engage the whole brain and invoke emotions; they get your reader involved and it's easy to link to the point in hand. You can demonstrate the cause and effect of something that has taken place. If you think about how many stories you use in day to day conversation, you'll see how important this is.

Let me share a story with you! In May 2014, I decided to attend the 'Speak like a TED Talker' event run by Ginger Training and Coaching (and hosted by Sarah Lloyd-Hughes, the author of *How to be Brilliant at Public Speaking*, who comes highly recommended!). This helped me to get clear on my story and journey.

When we were preparing for the event through a series of webinars prior to the weekend, I said that I wanted to talk about courage. The feedback I had on this topic was this: "Everyone talks about courage, what is your unique angle?" Hey, I don't always get it right!! So I decided to share my why; why I've developed the courage to run a business despite being an introvert, and also some of the inspiration behind it.

This led to me creating a 10 minute talk called 'Are you ready to die?' which I designed around the 'Hero's Journey' format. You are welcome to watch the video on my YouTube channel, although please excuse the shaky camera work, and I know that it's not perfect! What made this even more powerful is that I shared my Dad's story – I won't say anymore, so watch it and let me know what you think. You can go to the download section for the direct link: www.yourbookisthehook.com/downloads.

Only you know if your story is interesting enough for you to write a book about it. But to be honest, I didn't think I had a story until I went through this experience above, and it made me want to share it. Although it's not been an easy journey, and you'll probably understand this a little more when you read the next point.

Blocks and saboteurs that might stop you from writing your book

As I mentioned above, when you are writing your book, you'll probably be sharing some personal experiences. One of the problems that many of my clients face when exposing themselves in this way (or indeed in any way when you choose to stand out) is that you may feel vulnerable, especially when sharing your foibles, mistakes or weaknesses. But you'll probably find that when you do, people will empathise with you. Actually it makes you real rather than someone who says that life is peachy and nothing ever goes wrong! If this worries you, you need to get over this if you are actually going to publish your book.

When I wrote my first book I went through huge resistance and blockages which almost stopped me from publishing it. I'd interviewed some top names in the coaching industry and I knew I had important information to share, yet after writing the first draft, I started to question the content. I asked myself questions like:

- Who am I to write a book?

- What if people don't like it?

- What if it's no good?

- What will people think?

You might be wondering what helped me to get over myself in this situation, so upon reflection, this is what I did:

- I took a deep breath, felt the fear and did it anyway! I knew that some people wouldn't like the book and that was OK. But I also knew that if I didn't publish what I'd gleaned from these experts, I wouldn't reach the people who needed it.

- I set myself some deadlines to get back into the practicalities of publishing the book rather than the emotional connection behind the sabotage.

- I realised that if I wanted to create and develop the successful business I desired, then writing and publishing this book, and becoming more visible, was something that I simply had to do.

- I also knew that I'd feel terrible if I didn't write the book, as it was one of my dreams and I wanted to fulfil it. Yet I didn't realise that it would lead to more writing, as much as I love it!

Even with my book *The Mouse that Roared*, this has stalled a few times due to the vulnerability of sharing what has happened to me, and the mistakes I've made. But what makes it important is the fact that I've lived to tell the story! I call this my third book, but it has been on the back burner for a while, and it will be published after this one!

In my opinion, it doesn't matter that you're still on the journey that you are teaching to your readers. I vividly remember when I interviewed Blaire Palmer for my first book. We were sat in a busy cafe in Bath and she shared plenty of stories during those few hours. She told me about someone who had put her on a pedestal and saw her as this perfect person. But when Blaire shared with her a decision she had made personally, this lady realised that Blaire was human like everyone else, which is an important message to note. You really don't have to be perfect yourself – actually who really is perfect?!

Take a moment to learn from my friend Suparna Dhar, who has recently published her first book. In this short case study she shares the positive impact that writing it has had on her confidence and business focus.

Case study: Suparna Dhar, author of *Cooking Together: Step by Step Guide to Yummy, Healthy and Fun Recipes*

Over the last eight years I have supported mums who have experienced domestic abuse and helped them find the confidence to create a happy, healthy and fun family. I am a Coach, Trainer and Author.

In November 2012, whilst coaching a mum, I was inspired to write a children's cookery book with recipes shared by women who had been affected by domestic abuse, with proceeds going to Women's Aid.

Since publishing my book, my business has benefited hugely, as I have appeared in local newspapers and given talks, including being asked to speak and do a demonstration at Jamie Oliver's Food Revolution Day 2014. I have run cookery schools, spoken at networking groups, started a support group and been commissioned to run healthy eating programmes based on recipes from the book.

I have also started challenging myself in areas such as marketing, which is something I used to find difficult, turning down work and therefore freeing up time to focus and deliver work that is aligned to my business. The book has also helped me share what makes 'Life's Canvas' different, as this was much more than a cookery book; it was a real celebration of freedom and a way of mum and child building a bond together through cooking.

In addition, as an individual, real transformation has taken place. During the process of writing and publishing, I learnt that I could build excellent working relationships with a variety of professionals such as a food photographer and a graphic designer, work on a tight budget, focus on the dream and never give up. As a result I have gained a huge amount of confidence, learnt to accept myself and found a voice which had been suppressed for many personal reasons.

In a nutshell, writing a book has not only attracted new opportunities and will continue to do so, but it has increased my levels of confidence, positivity and authenticity in every aspect of my life.

Suparna Dhar
www.lifescanvas.co.uk

Lastly, I'd like to go back to the question posed at the beginning of this section: "Do I know enough to add to the millions of books already out there?" Only you know this answer. Although if you are using your book to share your expertise, I'd be surprised if the answer is no!

Things to think about

Focus on what makes you and your book different.

Get clear on your angle and hook that helps your book to stand out from the crowd.

Start to work on your story and how this is important in your book.

Know what might stop you from writing your book and how you can you get over this.

Action points to ensure your book is different

Research what else has been written on your subject and competitors in your industry.

Get clear on your topic before going to the planning stage.

Start to map out what you want to include in your book and how you might structure it.

Look at gaps in your knowledge and how you can plug these gaps.

To download a brilliant mind-map taking you through each step in this section in a visual way, remember to go to www.yourbookisthehook.com/downloads to view this blueprint and get access to all the other bonuses now.

Section 3

How to get started with your book

When I introduced the topic of writing and publishing a book, the question that most people asked was: "Where do I start?" As you've found in this book so far, there are two big topics to cover before you even think about getting started with your writing!

There is not much point in spending your time and energy writing your book, if you haven't nailed these important things first. Three of the mistakes that are easy to make are:

- Starting to write your book without a clue why you're doing it.

- Not knowing who your book is going to appeal to, or not aligning your book to your business.

- Not taking time to consider what people actually want to read.

The Summer Book-Camp helped me to get started. I asked people for their questions on writing and publishing a book, and I answered them live on the free webinars. The strategy behind this had four main intentions.

1. I was using the webinars to demonstrate my credibility and I wanted to share my expertise on writing and publishing a business book.

2. The Book-Camp was used as a lead magnet to grow my list and get noticed in this area by people who didn't already know me.

3. I wanted to find out what my readers' biggest challenges and questions were when it came to writing a book, so that I could answer them in this book and also do further research where there were gaps in my knowledge.

4. I wanted to run a six week programme alongside writing this book and promoted this on the webinars.

I did ALL of this before I even started to sit down and plan my book. Then once I'd sold the programme, I realised that I needed to get my backside into gear and start writing! It's amazing what a tight deadline does to get you focused, rather than putting it off for another day! Actually this is a process that I teach to my one-to-one clients and it enables you to monetise your expertise too. Feel free to contact me to find out how I can help you to put this into practice immediately.

Getting started is key, as is getting your book finished. I often come across people who have started writing a book, but it becomes so overwhelming that they don't know how to finish it – which is one of the reasons why this programme works. Or they find that something gets in the way that stops them from publishing it.

That's why in this section, I aim to get you started, help you to develop a master plan, and also give you strategies to keep you motivated and get your book completed too!

Chapter 7
How to plan your book

Before you put pen to paper, hand to keyboard, or mouth to Dictaphone, it is really important to plan your book. It's not enough to just start to type and hope it will all fit together. All this will do is result in ill-formed plans, a structure that is a little ropey, and you'll probably give up when it feels like you're getting nowhere fast with your writing.

Bring all of your ideas together

When you start, you might have all sorts of notes, scraps of paper, odd pieces of recorded thoughts, and ideas in your head that you've never written down. These might be spread all over your office or around your house, down the back of the sofa, or somewhere in your smartphone! Do you think that this will get you organised enough to write your book?!

 Top tip: Bring all of your notes, ideas and thoughts together before you do anything else.

You can start by creating a physical lever arch file for notes, or a dedicated notebook where you can write all of your ideas. If you like making notes electronically, create a folder for these on your computer, and if you do this, please make sure that you back up the information regularly or store it somewhere like 'The Cloud' or 'Dropbox'.

The latter will make it easier for you if you want to work on your thoughts when you're out of the office as well.

If you have ideas in your head, take time to write them down, type them up, or record them via audio instead. Here are a couple of resources that might help you during your book writing and planning stages:

- Use a note-taking app that you can download onto your smartphone. This means that if you are out and about and have a good idea, you don't have to wait until you get back to your office or have a pen and paper to write it down. 'Evernote' is a good tool, and you can also copy and paste your notes into Microsoft Word, an email, or sync the programme to your computer.

- If you feel more comfortable with speaking your ideas, this is another option to consider. 'Evernote' also allows you to do this as long as you have a microphone that picks up your voice. The only downside with this is that you will need to transcribe your ideas later, or you could use a transcribing tool like 'Dragon' to do this for you.

Then once you have all of your ideas in one place, it's time to put together your master plan for your book.

My favourite planning strategy

Although I am predominantly a logical, process-driven and planning-orientated person, there are times when I love to be creative. Planning a book is one of those times. When it came to developing my first book, I took out my flipchart, got a pile of sticky notes, and I wrote down all of my ideas on individual sheets. Once I had brainstormed everything I wanted to include in the book (there was a big pile of multicoloured ideas!), I started to plan it.

I looked at the themes that I wanted to cover, and I'd already got an idea of what these might be through doing my research. Then I started to stick them onto the flipchart under the relevant section. I added additional notes where I felt something was missing, or where I felt I needed to go into more detail. I also moved things around when I realised that something was in the wrong place.

What this planning allowed me to do was to develop a structure for the book, and avoid duplications that I'd worry about finding later – a key thing for me as I'd interviewed many people and it would be easy to do. I also wanted to be able to break my concepts into bite-sized chunks that felt easier to manage than the thought of writing a whole book!

Then after this I sat down at my laptop and transferred these ideas into a brief plan that I was able to type up and follow, but I kept my handwritten notes to hand to refer to when I needed to do so.

This is a process I use with many of my clients who engage me to help them to write their book. I rock up for our meetings with flipchart paper, coloured pens and lots of multicoloured sticky notes. We take plenty of space and time to brainstorm, develop ideas and concepts and get deep into the planning process to develop the structure for their book.

Another way in which you may wish to do your planning is to do a mind-map, and this is what I did for my second book. The reason for this was that I already had a clear focus. I had a signature system that I was sharing, and it made logical sense to turn seven steps into seven chapters. Although I also knew that the last chapter was a big one, and this eventually became four chapters when I created the sub-steps within this final section.

For this book, I took a different approach again. After all, this is technically my fourth book, and I've become pretty seasoned at this! I started with a blank Word document and brainstormed the process that I take when I write my books, and this became the bones for this book. Then I put the meat on the bones through developing the programme that accompanies this book, and referring to the questions asked during the programme. This became a detailed Word document that I effectively followed to write this book.

When I started each section of the book, I copied and pasted what I wanted to include in the chapter and used this to develop my writing further. This enabled me to keep on track and stay focused. Of course there were times when new stories came to me or I did a little more refining, but ultimately it helped me to write the first draft of this book in around five weeks and initially 33,000 words (and this was probably around 50 hours of actual writing). Of course, the more you do it the easier it will become, and – as you'll find out later – the writing is the easy bit!

Find the way that works for you when planning your book. Make sure that you have a structure first, as it will help you with your writing and motivation later.

Seven steps to write your book

Picture this now: You have your plan, and beside you might be a pretty collage of notes, multicoloured pen marks, words, headlines, illustrations and diagrams.

You open up a brand new Word document on your computer and you've told yourself that today is THAT DAY when you are going to start writing your book. You're sat behind your desk with that blank document staring back at you.

- Where do you go next?

- How do you start your writing?

Well I could say that you've got to start somewhere, and just write it. But that might not be so easy, so let me share a few tips.

1. Plan your writing

One of the questions I was asked in the Summer Book-Camp was: "How do you fit writing into your daily life?" There's not much point in choosing your busiest period and hoping that it will happen. Many people will go away to write their book, or they'll book some time away from their usual client work. That's what I have to do when I'm writing.

Let's be honest, unless you are really committed, you're not going to write your book unless you plan it in your diary, are you? And even if you do write it in your diary, is it actually going to happen?

My first piece of advice about writing is to work out when you are at your best. If you are a morning person and have your best ideas then, why not block out time first thing in your day? Of course you need to fit it around other things in your life, but I'm sure that you're more likely to do it if you know when it's going to take place.

If you do put the time in your diary, stick to it. Like some of my clients, you might commit to doing your writing at the same time every day. You may schedule a couple of hours in your diary and measure your success by the number of words you write or the amount of time you've focused on your writing. Personally I prefer to block out larger chunks of time in my diary, as when I schedule a couple of hours to write, other things invariably get in the way, or I find excuses that stop me from getting focused.

In September 2014, I took a group of my clients to South West Spain for a writing retreat. I initially created this opportunity because one of my clients kept telling me that she never had time to write. With the best intentions, she's often distracted by children who need to be taken somewhere, or other priorities get in the way. I felt that five days in the sun with plenty of time to write and be inspired, as well as one-to-one time with me, would be a great thing to do! The feedback that I received from the trip was amazing, and I've booked it again for 2015. Go to www.writingretreats.co.uk for more information and future dates, and to find out what my clients thought about the first retreat.

2. Turn off distractions

I recently wrote a blog post about my rules for writing, and one of the things that I have to do is turn off distractions. This means that my phones go onto silent, I close my email, and I shut down the internet unless I'm doing some research. Sometimes I have music on in the background, but usually I'll sit at my desk in silence and shut my door, and woe betide anyone who comes to talk to me!

I also like to write with a tidy desk. Sometimes I'll have my notes beside me, but generally a clear desk = a clear mind. Also when I get into flow, I tend to forget about time, so I'll often be sat there with a cold cup of peppermint tea and an empty stomach. Just do whatever you need to do to be comfortable and get focused.

3. Know what's next

I have to reiterate how important planning is to writing your book. Two of the questions that I was asked on the Summer Book-Camp were: "How do you keep writing when the ideas stop coming?" and "How do I overcome writer's block?" I touched on this a little earlier, so let me share my secret with you.

With my books, I always know what's next... If I haven't written for a week and I open up the Word document which is becoming my book, I have notes on the page about what is coming up next. If I've had to leave my writing mid-chapter, I'll have some idea of my focus without wasting time re-reading, re-editing, or having to think deeply about where to start. And I do just start. It doesn't matter if the first draft needs refining in places; it's all about getting going and doing the polishing later.

4. Write now, edit later

My preferred style of writing is to sit at my computer and type, and the most important thing that I have to mention here is that when I am writing, I never ever edit as I go. Imagine if you did this every time you wrote your book. You'd always be refining, perfecting and never moving forward. I might do a quick spell check when I'm writing, as I am a touch-typer and sometimes my fingers can't catch up with my brain! But apart from that, invariably I edit later unless I see a glaring mistake that I pick up from a quick glance.

Remember that these are my suggestions, and you don't have to follow them word for word, but I can tell you that this works!

5. Break it down into bite-sized chunks or mini-deadlines

Writing a book is a pretty big task. You're looking at creating many thousands of words and generating ideas too. So breaking your writing into bite-sized chunks or setting yourself mini-deadlines may be a way for you to go.

 Top tip: You don't have to write the whole book at once – unless you want to!

One of my clients is writing a book, and following our planning session, she decided to write her book as many smaller blog posts. This means that every time she writes, 500 words will start to create her book. This has a couple of benefits. Firstly, she can share the blog posts as she goes, so she can generate feedback and refine her message if necessary. Secondly, she can create a name for herself before she has finished writing it, and thirdly, it makes her book easier to write!

To get more inspiration in this area, let me share with you the story of Sandra, who took a very similar approach.

Case study: Sandra Peachey, author of *Peachey Letters – Love Letters to Life*.

I own and run LifeWork – a HR and Coaching Consultancy – and it always made a lot of sense to me that publishing a book raises your business profile and helps to establish you as an expert in your field. I even started to write not one, but two books, but never got around to completing them. However my writing *really* took off in 2012. I wanted to set myself a business challenge and decided to write a blog a day, every day, for a month. As a result I wrote a 'Love Letter to Life' every day for the Valentine month of February, to the people and phenomena that had shaped my life, showing people how to be their own best coach, and posted them on my blog www.peacheyletters.co.uk.

I started posting links to my blogs on social media and the response was immediate – from my very first published post, commenters were suggesting that I turn them into a book. During that month I published 29 posts and to my amazement created a following around the world, with my blog being read in 82 countries and having nearly 4,000 hits.

I then took this material and developed it into a manuscript. Using the blog, I had already established a loyal following and marketplace and in fact I used the myriad of positive comments I had received on social media as the introduction to my book.

My book was published in 2013. As a result I received PR I had only previously dreamt of, being featured in local press, as well as in *Psychologies Magazine*, a two-page spread in *The Lady*, and a number of appearances on BBC Radio. Not only this, but the book is now stocked in libraries across the UK too.

My book has definitely opened business doors in a number of ways. I have broadened the marketplace that I now appeal to, having got coaching clients directly as a result of reading the book; I have established my credentials as a coach; I am often asked to speak at networking groups, conferences, book clubs and even literary societies, and as a result I have the opportunity of introducing my audiences to the range of services that my company provides.

And this is all quite apart from the personal satisfaction of having published a book. It is, overall, an experience that I would highly recommend.

Sandra Peachey
www.peacheyletters.co.uk

6. You don't have to write your book

This is my process for writing a book, but if you don't find it easy to write, here are some other ideas.

If writing is not your thing, get someone to do it for you. There are plenty of ghost writers who will interview you, get to know you and help you to share your ideas by writing them for you. In working with you, they'll help to find your own unique voice – see the tip at the end of this chapter.

You could also record your ideas and get them transcribed. This is for you if you know that your greatest ideas come out through gems when you speak. Then you can always generate new content and ideas, even if you're not in your office.

7. Don't stress!

If you sit down to write and the words are not coming, despite putting all the planning into place, please don't stress. Although I find it relatively easy to get into flow, there have been many times when it feels like my writing is going nowhere. If this is the case, don't get worked up, just re-plan your diary, book another time to get focused and it won't be long before you are ready to get going again.

Although, if this is a regular occurrence, the next chapter is just for you! But before I move on, let me share some tips from Ginny Carter to help you to find your voice.

**Finding your voice
– Ginny Carter** gives you seven great ways to find your author voice

If you're like many budding authors, you'll have heard about finding your 'author voice'. This is the voice that's authentically yours when you write. And you do need to find it, because:

- If you come across authentically in your book, your readers are more likely to trust you.

- You'll write consistently if you write in your own voice.

- Your voice is unique to you, as are your ideas, passions and opinions. It will be one more thing that makes your book stand out.

- By writing as you, your book will come alive with your own personality. Your readers will come back for more.

The good news is that you already have a voice – you don't need to make one up! But how do you find it? Here are seven great ways:

1. Think of three words to describe yourself, e.g. 'bossy, funny, confident'.

2. When you're writing, speak to yourself at the same time. Imagine you're talking to the kind of person your book is aimed at, and translate the conversation into words on the screen. You may have to edit out some of your more colloquial words and phrases, but you will be writing as you.

3. Don't write any words that you would NEVER use in everyday life. Whatever words you would normally use, write those.

4. Eavesdrop on conversations around you, paying attention to the way people say things. Sometimes you'll want to borrow what you've heard because it sounds just like you; other times you'll think how you would have said it differently. Write these things down.

5. Pick five of your most popular blog posts, talks or social media posts. What jumps out in them as being 'you'? And what got a good response from your audience? Make a list of the ten words and phrases that are most and least 'you'.

6. Ask the people around you what words and phrases they always hear you use. You may be surprised! These words will be the bedrock of your writing character. You may not want to use all of them, especially if they're not suitable for a book, but they will give you a big clue as to how you come across. You can then work these words into your writing.

7. Read back what you've written a few days ago. Ask yourself if you would want to read it. If not, you're not writing in your voice.

Ginny Carter is a business book ghost writer who specialises in writing in your voice.

Email: ginny@marketingtwentyone.co.uk
Web: www.marketingtwentyone.co.uk

Things to think about

Get focused on the best time for your writing and plan it into your diary. Then make it happen.

Make sure that other distractions don't get in the way of your vision.

Break down the bigger goal into bite-sized chunks that make it easier for you to manage.

Just do it!

Chapter 8
What might get in your way?

In Chapter 6 I already touched on what might happen when you share your story in your book. Even without writing anything about you personally, when you make the decision to step up in your business, you will become more vulnerable than if you stay small and don't tell people about what you do. Of course, you might be the sort of person who is able to brush off criticism and not care what people think, or perhaps it concerns you and it may actually stop you from finishing your book.

In this chapter, I want to get clear on what might get in your way, because once you are aware of your triggers, it makes it easier to overcome them.

What do you think might get in your way when you are writing your book?

How to get out of your own way

As I've already mentioned, when it comes to getting in your way, the biggest thing that is likely to stop you is *you*. It is no coincidence that in my Seven Step Success System that I teach in my second book, the third and fourth steps are 'Cultivate your confidence' and 'Cut the crap'. As I've devoted two chapters to this topic, I'm sure you can see why these topics are relevant for many people who want to create a successful business.

It's not just the external criticism that might stop you; it could also be your internal voice. I've had a number of conversations with clients who have been all fired up about doing something and then they self-sabotage. They come up with excuses not to do something, or they find that something gets in their way and it's easy to put things off until later. Often there is nothing more to it than that internal dialogue stopping you from taking action.

If I take you back to the first section of this book when I talk about mindset, remember that 80% of your success is down to your way of thinking. Of course, having a great writing style is essential, but when you believe you can do it, won't let anything get in your way, and are brave, you are more likely to be successful and finish writing your book.

But you might find yourself questioning whether you know enough, whether you are good enough, and whether you are really an expert in your area. You might feel like a fraud, that you are going to be 'found out', or worry about what people might think when they read your book. How do I know? Well I've been through this myself, as I mentioned earlier in this book. But what I didn't explore then – and will do now – is why this happens.

I remember in my first book I shared statistics about 'fraud' or 'imposter syndrome', and up to 70% of people fear that they will be labelled as a fraud at some stage in their life. There is something that's going on that prevents them from believing in themselves. Often this doubt will be unfounded, and will be based on a fear or worry, despite all the evidence that points to someone who has knowledge and credibility.

 Top tip: You can do it! If you're struggling with this message, write down 10 statements detailing how your knowledge and expertise supports this affirmation.

That's when focusing on successes, achievements and results will help you to get over the things that might otherwise stop you. Instead of focusing on the things you don't know, concentrate on the things that have gone well; surround yourself with people who encourage you, and hold onto positive thoughts and triumphs.

Then, of course, there are the vulnerabilities and authenticity issues associated with sharing your stuff, especially if you feel that you aren't perfect, just like I mentioned earlier. But if this is you, what would happen if you didn't do this? What impact would it have if you kept your knowledge to yourself? Many of my clients teach what they've learnt themselves, often through their own experiences, and most people have a story that will inspire and teach their clients.

As Henry Ford famously said, "Whether you believe you can or you can't, you're right", so if there is something stopping you from starting or finishing your book, I suggest you explore that now.

I know that some people will get huge benefit from this book. It will give them the strategies, structure and motivation to write their book. I know that some people will find it less useful and may not like my approach, and that's OK. Although I'll never forget my first (and only) negative Amazon review, and like many people I ignored the other nine positive reviews and focused on this one instead! But I also know that unless I share what I believe is important, it won't inspire you to take action and create your own book to stand out in your business.

How to stay motivated to get your book finished!

If you are struggling to get and stay motivated, then go now and re-read Chapter 7 about planning. However, unless you are motivated to follow the plan, your writing will never progress further and you'll never get your book finished and published.

That's one of the reasons why I mentioned in the first section that you need to know why you are writing your book:

- What is it going to give you?

- What will it give your clients?

- How would you feel if you never finished it?

Which of these questions works for you will be determined by whether you are motivated by 'away from' or 'towards' strategies (e.g. you either prefer to avoid pain or discomfort, or you are motivated to achieve pleasure or success).

Another thing that you could consider doing is taking a moment now to project yourself into your future and do a little visualisation.

Imagine that you've finished your book; you've had it published and there is a knock on the door. Stood in front of you is a delivery driver who has a box for you. As you open this box, you see your book there and you suddenly have the first copy in your hands with your name on the front cover. How does this feel? What do you see? What do you hear? You can play with these feelings to intensify these emotions and make them stronger – strengthen your feelings, make the colours more intense and turn up the sound. You could also imagine yourself at your book launch, giving a talk that you've dreamed of, or something else that will inspire you.

Answering these questions or doing a visualisation may be the catalyst that keeps you motivated. They may keep you going when it feels tough, and you wonder why on earth you are sitting at your computer whilst everyone around you is fast asleep!

However, when there is no one on your back or giving you a kick up the backside when you need it, it will be more difficult to make it happen. That's why some of my clients engage my services, because that's what I do (but in a nice way!). Please contact me to find out how I can help you too.

If you seek external feedback, apart from having a coach or mentor, another thing you can do is to regularly share your writing with other people, get their opinion and then make changes accordingly.

Top tip: Get back in touch with the reasons why you are writing your book, and how you will feel once you have that copy in your hands or when your readers tell you what a difference it has made to their lives.

It's time to take your book off the back burner

When I ran the Summer Book-Camp, I was asked: "Have I left it too long on the back burner to start again?" This was asked by someone who I know and she had started her book five years prior, and I do believe that it's never too late. Of course, technology changes, opinions move on, but as long as you revise your material accordingly, it's never too late to write and publish your book. I am also pleased to be supporting this lady with her book and her business.

I also remember going to a book launch of one of the ladies who I interviewed for my first book, and one of the things that she said throughout her presentation was that her book had continually gone on the back burner. But finally we were there at her book launch. It didn't matter that it took a while to get there, as she had done it eventually!

If you have fears, concerns or are worried about your confidence, I suggest you check out my second book, *How to Stand Out in your Business*, as it's worth addressing these in your business generally, and I'm not going to repeat these strategies here. Although my biggest piece of advice is to just write your book! Then later you can refine it, get additional support to make it even better, and tweak it until it's the best it can be.

Things to think about

Know why you are writing your book.

Get clear on what might stop you from writing your book and then work out how to get over this.

Get out of your own way and believe in yourself.

Don't worry about your book being perfect at this stage.

Action points to get started with your book

Bring all of your notes and ideas together in a file.

Get planning. However you choose to plan your book, this is a vital part of writing your book and don't skimp on this area to get your book written.

Break down the tasks into manageable chunks and develop a timetable that works well for you.

Look at what may stop you from finishing your book and get support to make it happen.

If you are a visual person and would like to see a step-by-step guide to take you through this section, then go to my website to download this and plenty of bonuses to support you: www.yourbookisthehook.com/downloads.

Section 4
Bringing your book together

Imagine that you are sat at your desk with your plan and that you now have the confidence to get started!

You find that the words are starting to flow out of your head onto the paper or your screen and that you're bringing all of your material together.

You're focused and you find it easy to stick to your writing plan, and you're excited about what you are creating for your readers. You know that it's exactly what they want and occasionally you check in with them to confirm that you're still on the right path.

But there might be a few questions that you want to ask about what to include and how to bring your content together. You also might be starting to think about what's next in the book process and who can help you.

In this section, I'd like to share with you some tips on writing, bringing your book together and how you can make your book stand out.

I'm sure you can see that unless you bring your book together, your book will remain a dream; it will become an unfinished masterpiece, or go on that proverbial back burner. But the strategies I'll be sharing with you now will enable you to take the next step with ease.

Chapter 9
Strategies for writing your book

When it comes to writing your book, you might be willing me to share some strategies to actually put your words down onto paper. If you follow the process in this book, by now you should have some notes in front of you, and you should know what you're writing and in what order. Also I do hope that you are ready and raring to turn your ideas into text that your clients want to read.

You should have already done the ideas part, where you have poured out all of your thoughts into a plan. Then when you start writing your book, you are not distracted by other things you need to research or thoughts that need developing as you go.

The writing itself may feel a bit daunting, so in this chapter, I want to give you some quick and easy principles to follow. I'm sure that you want to create a book that is informative, yet easy to read. Perhaps you visualise the structure that you wish to create, the things that you want to include, and the key points that you want to get across to your reader. I'm sure that you also want to create editorial that is attractive, easy to read, as well as sharing the wisdom that your readers seek.

Eight essential book writing strategies

If you've had experience of writing before, such as articles for magazines, blog posts or even dissertations or essays, this may not faze you. But if this is the first time that you've created a piece of writing on this scale, I do hope these eight essential book writing strategies will help you. This builds on the planning tips that I shared in Chapter 7.

1. Create a book that is easy to read.

If you've already got a structure in place, then creating a book that is logical shouldn't be a problem. However, it's also important to lay out the text to make it easy for your readers to follow. Consider doing the following:

- Break up your text into bite-sized pieces with regular defined sections and chapters (just like this one), and headlines and sub-headlines which break up the text.

- Use **bold**, *italics* or <u>underline words</u> to make an emphasis or highlight relevant points.

- Include bullet points or lists in your writing as this makes more of an impact, rather than losing important points in sentences and paragraphs.

- Keep sentences short. Use punctuation where appropriate, and make sure that your writing reads well. One of the things that I'll often do is read my writing out loud, as this makes it easier to spot mistakes or sentences that don't make sense.

- Remember also to stick to one topic per section, as jumping around will confuse your reader (and probably you as well!).

2. Tips for your writing

As well as creating a book that's easy to read, you might be wondering how to actually write your book! You might be asking questions such as "How formal does it need to be?", "How long should a chapter be?" or you might be wondering if you have the right things to say.

The advice that I was given when I started was to write as I speak. To be honest, this took the pressure off me as there were no airs and graces when it came to what I had to say. I can literally type the things that come out of my head, without necessarily worrying about having to be too formal with my writing.

Another great tip that helped me was to write the introduction last. I know, strange, isn't it? But how can you talk someone through your book, and how to follow it, if you've not written it yet? How can you create a great first impression if you haven't brought all of your material together? Plus it would be easy to stare at a blank page if you don't know where to start. As I am writing this piece of text, my first chapter just states 'Insert here!' I'll focus on this later.

I'd like to remind you here to just start and worry about editing later. Get your ideas and words on paper, develop it as you write, and then you can get support when you need it.

One of the most important things that you need to consider when you're writing your book – or indeed any other material including talks and your website copy – is to appeal to the different learning styles of your readers. Here's a strategy that will help you further and will give you focus that may help you to start your book.

The 4MAT System and how it applies to writing

With your book, it's important to engage your reader from the start, so let me share with you a system that you can use; this is especially relevant in your introduction, synopsis or other material where you want to grab someone's attention from the first word.

The 4MAT system is made up of four areas that should be addressed in the order below, and when you ask the questions of yourself and then write your text, you should make an immediate impact.

Why?

Why should people be interested in your book?
What is it going to give them?
Why should they read it?
Give your reader some reasons for reading your book, tapping into the emotions and logical reasons behind it. You'll note that in the introduction of this book I talked about the reasons why you need to write your book but mainly about what would happen if you didn't do it.

What?

What are you going to teach your reader?
What are the important elements, sections or chapters?
Share some theory. Tell your reader more about your book and what's included (and possibly what's not included too) – you should have seen how I did this in the introduction.

How?

How does your book affect your reader and how can they use the information after reading your book?
What is the system or process that they can follow to get results?
Tell your reader more about the practicalities of what you are going to share and how they can apply it personally.

What if?

Remind your reader of the key messages in your book and what they will get from it.
You may also want to give guidance by suggesting how your reader may wish to read your book.
Tell people about the risks and benefits of taking the next steps with you.
This is the part where you tell people how they can relate the text in your book to the real world and how they can apply what they have learnt.

3. Share stories, examples and ideas

Real life stories – whether they are your own or someone else's story – are a good way of breaking up your text. When you share a story you tap into the emotion of an experience and it makes the concept that you are teaching transferrable into a real life situation. I mentioned this in more detail in Chapter 5, so feel free to refer back to this, and you'll see how I've used stories and case studies throughout this book.

There may be specific examples which help you to explain a complicated or unusual concept, or you may want to show how something works in practice. Feel free to use whatever tools you need to demonstrate what it is that you want to teach your reader.

4. Include exercises and additional checklists

In my first two books, I included exercises and checklists that readers could follow and refer to alongside reading the book. If you are creating a book that requires your reader to take action, I'm sure that you want them to do something with the information that you are teaching them.

You could also refer your reader to specific resources outside of your book. This may be a workbook or programme that you have developed, that may help them to take their new-found knowledge to the next level. Or you may also link to your website, where they can download additional activities to complete or audios to listen to. With these options you are adding value, and these are also ways to use your book to build your business – so watch out for more about this later. You'll also see that at the end of each chapter specifically, I'm referring you to additional bonuses and blueprints that will enhance your experience of reading this book and add more value too.

5. Ask questions

When you are writing a book, you are not getting immediate feedback from your reader. You can't see their facial expressions, you can't see any excitement or confusion, and you can't find out immediately what else they want to know. Of course, you can tell them how they can get in touch with you, but there isn't that two-way communication that you get when you are working with someone personally.

Your book has the power to change the lives of your readers, so why don't you ask them questions to take their learning to the next level? Questions that allow them to reflect, where they can work out how the information they've learnt is relevant to them, and what they need to do next.

If I could ask you one particular question right now to help with your book, what would it be? Please email it to me at karen@selfdiscoverycoaching. co.uk to get an answer!

6. Include images or illustrations

If you want to add interest to your book, why don't you include images, illustrations or pictures? As long as they are relevant, these can add a different dimension to your text. For example, you could include a figure with a question mark when you are asking a question, or have a particular image for an activity, link to additional resources or piece of advice (like my top tips!).

However, images and illustrations in your book will add to the printing cost, so what I've done in this book is to direct you to the visual blueprints of each section, which can be found at www.yourbookisthehook.com/downloads. I commissioned a friend of mine, Emma Paxton, to create these for me to make it easier for you, the reader, to see how the process works.

 Top tip: What else can you do to break up the text and make your book appealing on the eye?

7. Linking to other resources

There may be times when referring to outside resources, statistics or concepts is relevant to your text. If this is the case, please remember to reference these to your source. You may have noticed that I did this earlier when I was quoting a statistic. There may also be times when you need to seek permission from a person who has created a piece of work that you want to use. For example, when I used Robert Dilts' 'Neurological levels' diagram in my first book, I had to seek signed authorisation from him to use it. Luckily for me it didn't take too long to get permission, but bear in mind that doing this may take a while, so do it as soon as possible so that you don't delay your book.

Also be aware of copyright as I'm sure you don't want to infringe someone else's work. There is no hard and fast rule about the number of words, etc, so if you are quoting a few lines from someone's book, it may not be an issue. Or if you are quoting information which is in the public domain, you may not need to seek permission. Also, if you are giving your take on a particular model, this may be OK. But please, if you are in any doubt, ask for consent from the organisation or author of the work. If you are representing the work in a positive way, the author of the resource should be pleased to have you share this information in your book.

Here's a website that may help you: www.copyrightservice.co.uk.

8. What format will you use?

Lastly, before I move onto the next chapter and helping you to bring all of your work together, I'd like to briefly touch on what format you may use to create your book. I've already mentioned these in the book, but I'd like to bring the ideas into one place before I move on.

You may choose to teach a step-by-step system that readers can follow and implement, which is a brilliant way to share your expertise with prospective clients. You could also bring in interviews with other people, like I did for my first book, or seek other people to write chapters or sections for you. Or you could write it as a story rather than a 'how to' guide.

Things to think about

Keep your writing simple, consistent and easy to read.

Break up the text with chapters, sub-sections, lists, bullet points, and other relevant formatting.

Engage with your readers by sharing stories, exercises, checklists, and other appropriate information.

If in doubt, seek permission for any models or resources that you wish to include in your book.

Chapter 10
How to bring your book together

By this stage, I'd imagine that you have the first draft of your book, and you may have anywhere between 30,000–80,000 words in front of you. By the way, when I wrote my first book, I didn't have a clue how many words I needed to write. My first two books were both around 46,000 words, which is about standard for this type of book, and this one will be very similar. It certainly made it easier for me when I knew what this actually looked like when it was printed.

The most important thing is that you have covered the key points that are essential for your reader, it is in a readable format, and you keep your writing concise. It's not worth padding out the content with fluff just to make up the word count!

Four tips to get your book finished

When you are bringing your book together, there are many points to consider and I'll share some of these with you now.

1. Preparing your book

Unless you are typing your book directly into your publishing software, you'll need to think about preparing your manuscript. My preferred style is to write using Microsoft Word. Whilst writing, I like to see my script in 1½ line spacing as it enables me to print off chapters and edit at the end – and scribble adjustments in the margin. I also justify my text so that it makes it easier to read.

When I learnt to type, the norm was two spaces after every full stop, but etiquette has changed over the years, so you are likely to have one space now. However, consistency is key when you are completing your book for publication.

It's also important to consider your spelling. The norm (in the UK) is to use English (UK) spelling but the most important thing is to ensure consistency in all parts of your work, from comma spacing to hyphens, punctuation, number usage (e.g. one or 1), layout of bullet points and numbered lists, and anything else that is relevant.

2. Contents and headings

When you are publishing your book, having a contents page that is automatically generated will save you time. This is something that you can do within Microsoft Word, if you are using this software. Just use the Headings function within the Styles setting, and this will help you to generate a great contents page. This has the advantage that as you edit your book, the page numbers will change automatically when you refresh your contents page, rather than you having to do it manually with every single edit.

3. Editing your book

As I said earlier, I believe that writing your book is the easy part, because once you've finished the first draft, extensive editing will be involved.

When it gets to this stage, I'll print off the manuscript, read through it, and use a coloured pen to make notes. Then I'll go back to my computer to make the corrections. Then I'll probably do this all over again a few times!

There are different types of things that you need to do when editing. In the first edit you might be reading for sense, looking at what's missing and correcting any errors. Then once you've added in the missing elements, you might do various other pieces of editing – and it is easier to do these separately rather than check for everything at the same time.

- You want to check for readability and sense, and reading sections out loud will help you to do this.

- You may also wish to double check that you have not repeated yourself, although hopefully the planning will help you to avoid this.

- You need to check for consistency in terms of certain phrases you use and how you have set these out in your manuscript.

- You'll also want to check for consistency in spelling and formatting. You can see the formatting behind your text in Microsoft Word by using the ¶ button (paragraph marker). This will make it easier to review it on your screen.

One of the questions I've been asked is: "What is the cheapest way to publish your book?" Although I'm not covering publishing until the next section, there is an important point to acknowledge before I move on. If you are serious about writing a book, it's not worth being frugal. If you produce a sub-standard product complete with multiple typos and errors, what's this going to do for your brand?

Another question was: "What skills are required if my punctuation is not up to scratch?" This is an interesting question, as grammar is not my strong point. As I mentioned earlier, I do write as I speak, although on the plus side, people who know me can hear my voice as they read my words! And I'm also not afraid to start a new sentence with an 'and' even though this isn't technically correct! But if you are unsure about issues like punctuation, then these are things where an expert can help, as I will explain shortly.

Once you have the final version, you may have friends who are happy to give you their thoughts and advice. It is certainly worth having other people look through your text, to spot anything that doesn't read right and to tell you what they think. When I wrote my first book, my Dad read it from cover to cover and gave me important feedback as he was a stickler for grammar. You may also want to work with other experts to help you to develop and hone your manuscript.

As you'll be very close to the document itself, you don't want to skimp in this area as it's not always easy to see that typo or error, even if you are using the spell check function. It is very easy to miss an 'it' that should be an 'if' that your writing software may not pick up for you. It's also easy to misuse words like effect and affect, or practice and practise, and you may not always identify which one to use in each situation.

That's why I believe that it is essential to get outside support in terms of an editor and proofreader, and you will usually find that one person will fulfil both of these roles. This person is an essential part of your team, so who better to give you advice than my own expert! Here are some tips from Louise Lubke Cuss.

Finding the right editorial support for your book
– Louise Lubke Cuss tells you eight things you need to know about having your book edited and proofread.

1. You need someone objective. You won't be able to see your own mistakes. No matter how you may pride yourself on your spelling and grammatical abilities, chances are that some errors will creep through. In the end you will see what you want to see, and what you expect it to say. Editing checks more than purely errors, too.

2. Why you need an editor. The quality of your writing *is* important. Having your book edited and/or proofread is a quality assurance check for your book. You don't want reviews that say "Pity about the errors" – this may put off future

readers from buying your book. Errors detract from your message and credibility. Having your book edited or proofread is a necessary expense, if you want to be taken seriously.

3. You need a professional. You may wish to get people you know, who are experts in the field you are writing about, or a dab hand at grammar, to read your book to get their opinion, but please do also hire a professional editor/proofreader. They are trained in how to read texts for errors and are likely to pick up things that you haven't even noticed.

4. Editing vs. proofreading. You may not need an edit; you may only need a proofread. Editing is more costly than proofreading. An edit may include structural changes and suggestions, as well as corrections to grammar, punctuation, spelling and style, whereas a proofreader will give your work a final polish, eradicating any errors which have been missed, ensuring consistency of format and style, and only changing or querying things that are absolute clangers which, without attention, could spoil your book. You will find good descriptions of the difference between the two on the website of the Society for Editors and Proofreaders (www.sfep.org.uk). In my experience, most books require a "proofedit" which is a bit of both!

5. Make a good choice. Choose someone that is recommended by someone you know, has

professional qualifications, and belongs to a professional organisation, like the Society for Editors and Proofreaders (which has a searchable directory). Ideally, you want someone who is all three.

6. Ask for a sample. If you're not sure about who to choose, ask for a short sample of their work (using a few pages from the middle of your book). This will do three things: (1) give you an idea of the quality of their work, (2) give you a better idea, if you're new to the process, of what an editor will do, and (3) give the person doing the sample an idea of whether you need an edit or proofread, which helps them to quote accurately.

7. Editorial work isn't free. You won't get your book edited or proofread for nothing. You wouldn't expect to have a leak repaired for nothing, or a filling in your tooth, so why would editing a book be any different? You are paying for a professional service. However, if you are on a very tight budget, you may find someone who is fairly new to the profession, and thus willing to do it for a negotiable rate in exchange for a testimonial. That said, still choose a reputable professional – see (6) above.

8. Self-edit first. You can help yourself and your editor/proofreader by self-editing your book first, before sending it to your chosen professional. You will find plenty of advice

about this by searching on the internet, using keywords like 'self-editing tips for non-fiction'. Some things you might like to consider are: reading aloud to check that it sounds right, and flows, and checking that you have good links within your book to what has gone before and what's coming next.

Louise Lubke Cuss is an editor and proofreader, and lover of books!

Email: louise@wordblink.com
Web: www.wordblink.com

To reiterate what Louise is saying, a good editor/ proofreader will ensure consistency in your spelling, words, grammar, punctuation and formatting, and make suggestions to improve your text. They will also check that the final version is correct and ready for publication. Although remember that ultimately signing this off is up to you, and you need to make sure that you are absolutely happy with the final copy.

I believe that it is important to get the right people supporting you in your book. If you try and do everything yourself, you'll miss the things that are important. You'll be doing this, rather than the stuff that you are good at, and (I believe) your final product won't be as good as if you get other people on board to get it right.

4. Typesetting

If you go down the self-publishing route (more about this later), getting a designer to professionally typeset your book is important. Yes, it is another expense, but having a well-laid out book will help your credibility.

A book with plenty of white space will make it easier for your reader to follow your content, and it will look much better once printed too. If you upload your own book to a self-publishing tool, you may find that you have squashed margins, the format may change and your book may not look as professional as you had hoped when you started.

Actually I'm starting to talk about how you need to stand out with your book, so let's focus on this next.

Things to think about

Start with the end in mind when formatting your book. Consistency is essential in the language you use and the layout that you choose.

If you're using Microsoft Word, get to grips with the formatting tools (or those of your preferred system), as a well-laid out manuscript will help those who are supporting the publishing of your book.

Find a reputable editor/proofreader who matches your requirements, and can help you to perfect your book.

Ask for recommendations of people who can support you (and read on to the Publishing section for more advice on this).

Chapter 11
How to make your book stand out

When it comes to making your book stand out, it's got to look great. It needs to be a high-quality product, and with content that your audience wants to read. But it's not just about the formatting inside that's important, or the way you lay it out for your reader, it has to get noticed before someone even opens the cover.

Although you may be writing a book to promote at events, through your website, or as an information product, this chapter is equally important. Since many people will make a buying decision based on what your book looks like, you need to read on.

If you write a business book that blends into the crowd, one that is the same as all the other books available on your topic, then it's not going to be worth starting. If you have written 50,000 words that are similar to other publications, then go back to Chapter 1!

However, creating a book that stands out – when you follow the principles in this book – isn't difficult. In this chapter, I'll be addressing the areas you need to follow to help you to get your book noticed!

How to nail your book title

You may have wondered whether I was ever going to talk about nailing your book title. But if you focused on this first, would you have ever written a single word? Of course, you may have a working title, and be using this to guide your work. For this book, I had something happen to me that I've never had before. Before I'd even started to write this book, one of my friends helped me to create the title. But that's certainly unusual!

The thing about your book title is that it will help your book to stand out – as long as it is the right title (and subtitle). Being clever won't always work. Even if your title means something to you, it may not mean anything to your ideal readers – or what they might search for on Amazon.

Some popular books have included 'How to...' or '10 steps to...' Other successful books have short and snappy titles that quickly attract the attention of the potential reader. Your title needs to give people an indication of what they will get from the book or at least allude to the content. You want it to be relevant, memorable and easy to understand.

Also, don't be afraid to be controversial or rude. A very memorable series of books are the 'F**k It' series by John C Parkin, which is branded to the business of the same name.

 Top tip: Get feedback from people in your target readership to hone your title.

When I wrote my first book, I sat down and brainstormed around 6-8 titles, and then I sent these proposed ideas to trusted friends in the coaching industry to get their honest feedback. I asked them to vote A, B, and C on their top three titles and the winner was 'The Secrets of Successful Coaches'. This became the title of my first book.

Sharing my personal experience, this title had advantages and disadvantages. It included the keyword of my biggest target market – coaches – but on the downside, the content was equally applicable to business owners in other professions, as was often pointed out to me by some of my readers.

A good place to start is by considering the keywords that your readers may type in to a search engine to find your business or your book. If you are already running a successful business, you may have already focused on keywords in your website copy, your online marketing or when writing blog posts.

There are generally two types of people in this world in terms of how to find you online: one who knows what they are looking for, i.e. they know they need a hypnotherapist who specialises in stress. The other may know they need help with something (e.g. they may type in 'help with stress') but they don't know who can provide it. If you choose the right keywords, then your business or your book are more likely to come up in the results.

With your book, although you may not be thinking on such a deep level, take some time to really get clear on what your book is about and what someone may search for to come across your masterpiece.

Although you may be using your book as a positioning tool, I do hope that you will attract new followers through your writing. So you need to ensure your book stands out. Here are a few questions to ask yourself.

- If you were to read your book for the first time, what is it actually about?

- What are your readers going to get from it?

- What keywords relate to this content?

- How does your proposed title reflect this?

If you're struggling, check out some of the keyword tools on the internet, which may help you to come up with some ideas.

Don't forget you can also have a subtitle which tells people more about your book and what they will get from it.

Lastly, I want to remind you not to stress over getting your title right first time. You could spend days, weeks or months agonising over the right words, and never get your book started. One of my books has had numerous reincarnations in terms of its title, and I know that it can take time before you suddenly have that spark of inspiration!

Create a great book cover

Traditionally a book cover has been your first chance to connect with your prospective readers, and create a great first impression. This was in an age when you would go into a bookshop and peruse the shelves in your chosen genre or category.

Certain books would stand out and some would blend into the crowd. But even now with the online generation, it is also important to ensure that your cover gets noticed. It allows you to convey your message, potentially generate an emotion, and draw people towards your book.

For all of my books, I have used someone to design the cover for me, and I'm certainly not an expert in this area. The colour, font and images will have different effects on different people, although when you know your ideal reader, it makes it easier for you to create something that will appeal to this person. You may also want to consider your brand colours as ultimately your book is part of what you do. You'll need to make sure the font is easy to read and doesn't detract from your message.

For the artwork on your cover, of course you could have a picture of you – or you may prefer to leave this for the back cover! If you are looking for an image that depicts the message in your book, you have a couple of options. You can buy a stock image off the internet, however this will not be unique to you or your book, and you also need to check the copyright of your purchase before you use it. This is important whichever image you choose to use. The alternative is to commission someone to design a bespoke image for you or use a relevant photograph.

Ultimately it needs to be distinctive; the image needs to reflect your message, and engage with your ideal reader. For example, if you identified in Chapter 2 that your ideal reader is a woman in her early thirties who suffers from stress, then an image depicting a flustered woman or a lady in a zen-like state may be relevant. If you have lots of ideas, why don't you ask a designer to generate a few sample covers for you and get people in your target readership to tell you which one they like the best?

One last thing about your cover, remember that when the image is online it will be a fraction of the size of your actual book, so don't overcrowd the jacket if you want it to stand out.

Making an impact with your back cover

In the next section, I'll be talking about creating a synopsis or pitch for your book. This will help you to promote it to publishers, and it will also help you to write the short and snappy copy for your back cover.

The back cover is your pitch for the book. It needs to be impactful, punchy, engaging and tell your reader exactly who the book is for. In my second book, I talked about the principles of AIDA (Attention, Interest, Desire, and Action) and these principles can apply here too. For example, to attract your reader's attention, your copy might start with a series of questions, engaging with the struggles that your reader is going through. Then later, you will give your reader plenty of benefits to help them to make the decision to buy your book.

I'll expect you to also include an introduction to you, the author – by the way, as you are using your book to stand out in your business, I'm assuming that you'll be writing this under your own name rather than a pseudonym. You'll also then include some information about your credibility and why you've written the book. Although this probably won't be long in terms of the amount of text, as you don't want to crowd the cover with words. You also may choose to have a picture of you on the back cover (if you haven't decided to put it on the front!). You also may have reviews and endorsements, but more about that in a moment.

From a formatting point of view, there may be bullet points breaking up the text, and headlines, words in bold or italics and lots of space.

In addition, there are the statutory requirements including the ISBN number, publisher and the price of the book too. I'll cover this in the next section.

 Top tip: Why not look at some of your favourite books and see how other authors approach this section? Popping into your local bookstore or scanning through your bookshelf will make a good start.

How to get outstanding endorsements

Getting endorsements for your book includes both the foreword, as well as reviews that you may wish to include inside your book or on the back cover.

Having respected people in your profession endorsing your book is a great reflection on your brand and reputation. These are likely to be reviews from people who already have credibility in the mind of your audience. Although these don't just have to be famous people or notable figures in your industry, the right endorsement could have an incredible impact upon the success of your book.

For your foreword, the first thing I'd consider is, who is credible within your industry and who would you love to write it for you? For both the reviews and the foreword, if I simply said that you needed to write a list of these people and ask them, what would you say?

For *The Secrets of Successful Coaches*, I asked Peter Thomson, a well-respected figure in the business field, to write it for me, and he accepted the challenge. For my second book, I approached Rachel Elnaugh, formerly of *Dragons' Den* and Red Letter Days, to provide me with her endorsement. Both of these people wrote glowing testimonials for my books, which supported their credibility. Although I'd met both of these people personally, I contacted Rachel via Twitter because I know that she loves using this medium to connect.

Although having a foreword for your book is not essential, I believe that it gives your book credibility and authority. And if the people you contact are too busy or reluctant to write the foreword for you, why don't you give them a few ideas to help them write it. Plus, you can send them an overview or synopsis, and a few chapters if necessary.

If someone says no once, don't be afraid to go back to them later. Contact them via social media, their agent, or someone you know who is connected with this person who can recommend you too.

- Who would you like to write your foreword?

- Who could endorse your book?

- What do you want people to say about your book?

Create a compelling contents page

Lastly, you want to create a contents page that is compelling. If your ideal reader is browsing through your book (for example using the 'Look Inside!' feature on Amazon), you want the chapters and sections to be interesting and appealing. You want them to grab the reader's attention. This is a vital part of bringing your book together.

Things to think about

It's not just your writing that is important; your book needs to be noticed visually. Understand what makes your book stand out and how you can get this message to your readers simply and distinctly.

Start with a working title and you can always agree your final title later.

Engage someone to provide your artwork and make sure your cover – both front and back – stands out.

When you're ready, get endorsements from people you respect.

Action points to bring your book together

Write your book in a compelling way that will engage with your ideal reader.

Break up the text with other information that will support the text in your book.

Remember that you will be using your book as a marketing tool, so include other strategies to take readers from the page to your website or another resource.

Get support to make your book stand out when it is published.

To download your blueprint of this section, go to my website, where you'll also get access to new information that will help you to write your book. Here's the link:
www.yourbookisthehook.com/downloads.

Section 5
How to get published

Getting your book published is much easier now than it ever has been in history, due to the range of options available to authors. This is despite the fact that more books are being published, anyone who wants to be someone is writing a book, AND there is more competition for readership. As long as you're following these steps, you'll be writing the right book for your clients, and even if there is competition, your unique hook will help it to stand out.

Yet when it gets to the publishing stage, many people get stuck here. It can be a minefield, and that range of options may make it feel overwhelming. You've got to make a choice about how you want to get your book published, printed and distributed, without it distracting you from finishing your book either!

Technology has certainly paved the way, with many authors favouring the Kindle route without ever getting a single copy of their book printed. Also, you could go down the e-Book route where you use other forms of technology to allow people to view your book online.

Whether you are seeking to go down the traditional route, want to work in partnership with a publisher, get your book self-published, or want to publish online, you get to choose how to approach this part of the process. If you want help in navigating through this publishing maze, then you're in the right place.

Like many things in life there are advantages and disadvantages to each method, so I'd like to give you the opportunity to make an informed choice and take the right step for you.

However, before you even consider publishing your book, there's one more step first, and that is creating a great pitch for your book. Developing a clear and concise synopsis is going to help you to approach publishers, and assist you in the promotion for your book. This will be the sales tool that helps you to articulate your message, and will demonstrate how your book stands out from everything else that has been written on your topic.

It will give you an elevator pitch to approach people for endorsements, and it will help you to get clear on what you want your book to say about you. It will also enable you to write an amazing back cover, and ultimately sell your book. So this is the first step in this section, and then I'll get onto publishing.

Chapter 12
Create a powerful synopsis

Creating an effective sales pitch for your book is essential to get your book noticed. This document is known as a synopsis and the definition of this is "a brief summary", "an outline of a play, film or book" and that's exactly what you'll be creating here.

 Top tip: Get really clear on what people will get from your book and why you are writing it, as this gem may become the hook to nail your synopsis.

Why you need a good pitch

A good synopsis will sell your ideas. This is especially important if you are planning to approach traditional publishers or you want your manuscript to be given serious consideration by an editor or agent. Also your synopsis will give them a feel for what you have to say and how you write. This means that a clear, concise and well-worded piece could make or break their decision on whether to publish your book.

Even if you are not planning on submitting your manuscript to a traditional publisher and have decided to publish by yourself, creating a high-quality synopsis for your book will give you many benefits, so don't skimp on this process. It will support your marketing, facilitate your pitch, and give you the structure to sell your ideas to your clients and readers. It will help you to:

- Bring all the salient points from your book together into an engaging and succinct page or two that engages with your prospective reader.

- Make the reader feel curious about your book and what they can learn from reading it.

- Create intrigue from the start, so it needs to engage immediately without any waffle.

- Get clear on why your book is worth reading and why you're the right person to write it.

- Get to know your book intimately, which puts you in a better place to promote it.

You need to make sure that your writing is simple to understand and unambiguous, free from jargon, and not too wordy! Imagine you were giving an elevator pitch for your book, and start from there.

How to write a great synopsis

If you're with me so far, but you're still struggling to see where to begin, here are some tips to write a great synopsis.

1. Your proposed title and name

You need to start your synopsis with your proposed book title and your name. Although this may seem obvious, it's amazing how easy it is to forget this.

2. Short summary introduction

In the first section you want to give a brief outline of your book. Just like you were giving a great elevator pitch, now's the time to engage with the reader right from the very beginning. Don't start by telling people about you and what you've done or go on about your experience... You want to grab your reader's attention now.

Start with your hook. To make a great first impression start with a strong and powerful description of your book – and of course, what makes it stand out. Then you can continue to explain what's included in the rest of the book, but be clear on sharing the salient points right from the start, rather than them getting lost in the last paragraph.

In this section, once you've made a great impact, if pitching to a publisher, it would be useful to list competitors in your field. It would also be effective to outline why your manuscript is different, and where there is a gap in the market for this book. Also make sure you include two or three reasons why you are the best person to write it. If you have marketing opportunities that will support the book's launch, then include this information too.

3. Chapter overview

Including a summary of your proposed chapters will also help you to get across what you are covering with your book. Just keep your descriptions short and snappy, with a few lines or sentences for each chapter, including your proposed chapter headings.

Again, engaging the reader is essential, so the most important points need to stand out.

4. Details of your target reader

Next, you may also wish to include a short summary of your ideal reader and who your book aims to target. When you give an overview of your market, why not include some facts, figures, statistics or other snippets of information that demonstrate why your book is essential. Just remember, again, to be clear and concise.

5. Your biography

You'll also want to demonstrate your credibility in relation to your book by including a brief biography demonstrating your experience, your expertise and knowledge. Of course, when your book is aligned to your business, this bit should be pretty easy. Include anything that you feel would be valuable to prove your authority – be explicit and don't assume that your reader will understand something that you feel is a given, because it won't be.

You could also include successes, awards or accomplishments that you have achieved. Mention public speaking appearances, and any exposure you've had in the media, for example on TV, in newspapers or magazines. Also include any past books or publications that you have written. If you have any connections who will help you to promote your book (and this has been confirmed), this may also help your submission.

6. Your contact details

Lastly, remember to include your contact details, so the person reading your synopsis can easily get in touch, and this allows them to find out more about you too. Including details of your social media contacts, if you have a strong online community, may also sway the decision made by a publisher. This will also be useful if you are sending the summary to someone who you wish to endorse your book for you.

When to write your synopsis

Now you have the outline in place, you might be wondering when you should write your synopsis. You don't have to write it at this stage in your book writing; you can do it at any time, although it is easier when you have the outline of your book on paper. For example, if you were pitching your ideas to a traditional publisher you are unlikely to have finished writing your book before you do so. But you'll have a clear plan and probably a few chapters completed that you would submit alongside your pitch. If this is the case, you also may wish to tell the publisher or agent how far you have progressed to date, the proposed finish date for your manuscript, and how long it is likely to be in terms of the word count.

One final thing about writing your synopsis, make sure you write in a similar style to your book. It's especially important to get it professionally edited and proofread, as you only have one chance to make that great first impression!

To download a free template to help you to create your synopsis, go to www.yourbookisthehook.com/downloads.

Things to think about

Your synopsis is an important part of your writing and it will support your book's success, so don't hold back.

Being clear on what makes your book stand out is essential to know by this stage.

Don't be coy about your achievements or the claims you make with your book.

Remember that you've only got one chance to make a great first impression!

Chapter 13
Navigate the publishing maze

When you start thinking about publishing your book, you might be wondering where to start, who to approach, or what to do. It can be a minefield, as there are many different options available. You might be wondering which one is best for you and worth pursuing. Or you may simply have a mental block about publishing and would like advice about how you can reach your audience.

I must admit when I started out with my first book, seeking a publisher, and working out how to distribute my book, almost put me off finishing it. It seemed a complicated process, with many hoops to jump through. In this chapter, I'd like to set out all the choices for you – so that you don't have to do the same!

 Top tip: Don't spend months worrying about publishing, which stops you from writing your book!

Please bear in mind that through this book, my job is to help you to stand out from the crowd, and use your book as the hook that enables you to grow your business. I want to enable you to leverage your expertise, use your book as a positioning tool, so this is reflected in my thoughts and suggestions.

I'll outline the various options, tell you a bit more about them, and then give you what I think are the pros and cons of each choice. I've also included a few stories of mine and other people's experiences.

How to get a publishing deal

When most people write a book, their main goal is to get their book snapped up by a traditional publisher, and this is the first option I'll be mentioning in this book. Up until relatively recently, this was the main way in which any author could get their idea in print and then supplied to their reader.

What typically happens in this situation is that the author will complete their manuscript (or start to develop it at least), write a proposal or synopsis, and then send this proposal to a publishing house with a covering letter and a couple of completed chapters.

The editor at the publishing house will read it and decide whether to reject or publish the manuscript. If the latter is decided, then the publishing house will buy the rights to the work, and pay the author an advance based on future royalties.

The author will complete the book, which will be edited by the publishing house. Then the house will pay for the book design, package the final product and market the book on behalf of the author. All the expenses are paid for and the author gets royalties when the book sells.

What also might happen is that the author may contact an agent who will represent their interests and help them to get their book published. The author will still need to pitch their book to the agent and convince them of why their book is different. The agent will take commission from the book's royalties.

In reality, though, it is certainly not that simple.

Not many authors are accepted by a traditional publisher or can find a suitable agent. If you think of how many thousands of books are written each year and how few are accepted for publication, this process rarely gets further than the rejection step.

However, if you are really committed, let me give you some of the pros and cons of going down this path.

Advantages

- There is a particular kind of kudos when you are published by a traditional publisher that may help with marketing you and your book.

- Traditional publishers will support you with the editing and preparation of the manuscript, so you don't have to do everything yourself or need to source the right people. This also takes the pressure off you when they handle this crucial part of the process.

- They may give you a monetary advance – but be prepared to use this towards your marketing budget!

- The publishing house takes 100% of the risk of actually publishing your book, as they pay for the printing and publishing costs.

- You are more likely to get mainstream exposure if the publisher promotes your book with the same enthusiasm as you!

- Other opportunities may arise such as your book being published in multiple languages to give it a wider reach.

Disadvantages

- You need to create a highly developed proposal and manuscript to make it into the acceptance pile, and stand a chance of getting your book published in this way.

- If you are an unknown author with no national presence you are less likely to get a book deal.

- It can take many months or years to get your finished book into the public domain, so if you are using your book to raise your visibility, be mindful of this fact.

- Your advance and share of any profits are likely to be low, unless you are already well known and in the public spotlight.

- You will have minimal control over editing, and have to abide by the style preferred by the editor and the publishing house.

- You are less likely to be able to promote your other services throughout the book.

- Although you will get the support of a

publishing house, you'll still be doing much of the marketing yourself.

- The publisher holds the rights to your book and copyright, which may mean that it's not so easy for you to use your material in other ways, for example if you wish to re-write and re-publish your book later on.

- Ultimately it is not easy to get a traditional publisher to accept your book, and the process of doing so can be a time and energy drain.

I've had many conversations with fellow business owners who have gone down this route, some of whom have had success, and others who wish they'd chosen an alternative route. One such person told me that despite publishing through this method, in reality they've sold hundreds, not thousands of books, and have had to do much of the marketing themselves. However, here are some tips to help you through this process.

Traditional publishing tips

- Get hold of an up-to-date copy of the *Writers' and Artists' Yearbook* to get current details of publishing houses, agents and contacts, and their preferred method of submission. If you fail to meet their requirements, your work will automatically be rejected, and you don't want to be added to the slush pile of unsolicited manuscripts.

- Incidentally, the *Writers' and Artists' Yearbook* is also a great source of other advice and ideas about writing, publishing and marketing your book, even if you go down the partnership, self-publishing or Kindle route.

- When you are choosing a publishing house, check out what else has been published in a similar genre or category to your book. These are the first places to target as it is important for you to find the right fit for you and the publishing house.

- Your synopsis that I talked about in the last chapter is even more important if you are taking this route. It needs to be highly polished and accompanied by a covering letter that sells your book to the publisher. This needs to tell them why your book is worth publishing and why they are the right publisher to do this.

- In any correspondence it is important to outline your competitors' books and what makes yours different. You, an agent, or a publishing house needs to be confident that there is a market for your book.

- Go to the Annual Book Fair in London (or similar if you are not in the UK) as this will give you the opportunity to connect with publishers, agents and other people in the book writing and publishing community. This is useful irrespective of which publishing route you decide to take.

If you're not sure whether taking this traditional route is right for you, I'd like to share the experiences of two authors who have done this, and with very different results. Then I'll give you other options to get published.

Case study: Penny Pullan, author of a number of published books

I always felt I'd be a writer but never thought it would happen in the way it did! Not everyone starts with a pile of rejections...

My name is Penny Pullan and I work with people who are grappling with tricky projects, where tricky means ambiguous requirements, demanding people and virtual teams. I work with other consultants, and one of my colleagues was already an author. She came to one of my events and realised that my work complimented hers in a new way. She suggested we wrote a book together, and after a chat with her publisher and an accepted proposal, my first co-authored book was born, and published in 2011.

A year later, I took a call in my office from Kogan Page keen for me to write a book on Business Analysis. I very nearly turned them down, as I'd only just recovered from the first one! Thankfully I had the sense to consider it, and turned to a friend with publishing experience who told me in no uncertain terms to accept it! This time we agreed on an edited book with another co-editor and 26 contributors. It was as much hard work as writing the first book! However, we had a lot of fun working together as a team, and the book has sold well. The next three books are currently forming in my mind.

The advantages of traditional publishing have been:

- The book is proofread and produced for you with no upfront monetary investment.
- I've received advances each time and royalties afterwards.
- My books have looked and felt beautiful when I received them.
- It's easy to gain speaking engagements as a published author.

The disadvantages have been:

- Even at the author's discount, I have to pay a lot for each book I buy.
- I can't choose the cover design, although I have given a lot of input!
- I am not free to use the words I have written elsewhere without agreement from the publisher.
- Last year's royalty cheque paid for a Chinese dinner for my family.

Dr Penny Pullan
www.makingprojectswork.co.uk
Co-author of *A Short Guide to Facilitating Risk Management*
Co-editor of *Business Analysis and Leadership: Influencing Change*
Contributor to *The Gower Handbook of People in Project Management*

Case study: Emma Sargent, author of a number of published books

We have a book that is in the top 5% of selling non-fiction books and sold 10,000 copies in its second month when it was 'Book of the Month' in WH Smith airport shops. The average non-fiction book sells 2,500 books in the course of its lifetime, so that puts those figures into perspective.

It has been translated into 12 languages now and every few months we get a royalty cheque and copies of the latest translation – we have a heaving bookshelf of books that we can't read! It has sold reasonably well since then and we have made probably £15,000 from it.

We might be forgiven for thinking that it has been quite an achievement. Other people certainly tell us so.

However, that achievement also ranks as one of our biggest mistakes.

Let me explain. It's great (and useful) to have authored a published book, especially one that was published by a well-known publishing company. But like many business authors, we actually made a huge mistake. So what was the mistake? The mistake was that we didn't spend a single minute thinking about the outcome for us in having this book and what we wanted the book to do for us.

141

How on earth did that happen, I hear you cry?! It happened because I was working on my second parenting book, and knowing our area of expertise in business (communication), my editor invited us to write the book that later became *How you can talk to anyone in every situation*. We were flattered. What's not to like about being 'invited' to write a book? Plus, we had so much material, and had learned so much about book writing, that we were able to crack it off in about four months. However, that is still four months where we could have been doing something a lot more useful.

We are sorry to report that that book does precisely nothing for us, in terms of our business. It's obviously related to what we do and is more related to our corporate work, but does it get us clients? No. Is it a good book? Well, some would say it is; and isn't that just a matter of opinion?

A good book is simply one that a lot of people want to read and one that helps you to get business. A good book is one that lasts the test of time – that keeps selling over as many years as possible. But mostly a 'good' book is one that gets you business. And it gets you business because it carries the essence of you and what you do.

It is, and needs to be, your 'hook'.

Emma Sargent
www.theextraordinarycoachingcompany.com

Co-author of *How you can talk to anyone in every situation*
Author of *Flying Start: Coaching your children for life*
Author of *Brilliant Parent: What the best parents know, do and say*

Partnership publishing – the pros and cons

The second option you could consider is partnership publishing. This is the route I took with my first book. After months of spending time sending my manuscript to some of the personal development and business-focused publishing houses, this felt like the best option.

Partnership publishing is known as 'serious self-publishing' and bridges the gap between traditional publishing and doing everything yourself via the self-publishing route.

Basically you work in partnership with a publisher who will support you each step of the way to get your book to your readers. For example, they will help you with the production and distribution of your book, but you pay for the privilege of using them.

Here are some of the advantages and disadvantages of using this method. Please note that due to the vast array of different companies now supplying this service, this is purely based on my own experience, and may vary depending on the organisation you choose.

Advantages

- You get support to publish your book, which means that you don't need to do everything yourself. You pay them to do this part for you once you've finished your manuscript. This will often include a range of services, like editing, proofreading, typesetting, cover design, etc, some of which may be purchased separately or as part of a more comprehensive package.

- You don't have to worry about putting your book together, creating artwork or preparing your book for printing, although you will have input into this process.

- They will manage the distribution of your books, and pay you sales commission for every copy which is sold (less the percentage that they may take).

- They will also do the legal side of publishing for you, including registering it with the British and other libraries and providing the book with an ISBN number (more on this later).

- You will maintain control over the rights of your book. This means that you can do whatever you like with your book and the material, rather than having to work within the constraints set by a publishing house.

- You may be able to sign up for a marketing package, which will support you when your book is initially published (although see the notes below).

Disadvantages

- Partnership publishing can be a costly process when you add together all of the different elements to complete and distribute your book.

- You will often have to decide in advance how many copies of your book you wish to have printed, and it is easy to overestimate this. Although some will offer a print-on-demand service, but this will be more expensive than a larger print run.

- Depending on the company, you may not get editorial advice, and some companies will accept your manuscript without giving you feedback on how you can improve it.

- Even if you go for the marketing package (if offered), you will still need to do much of the marketing yourself – although this applies to every single option!

- Your publisher will take a percentage of your book sales, although the income from selling your book is likely to be higher than going down the traditional route.

If you are looking for a middle-ground method, partnership publishing is a good route to take. You will get the support to make the process easier for you. Although having done it the first time, I still decided to do it all by myself for book number two! This is because I'd gained more experience of the processes involved and felt I had the right contacts to do it this way.

Partnership publishing tips

- Any form of self-publishing (including partnership) has been known as vanity publishing in the past, although it is now a more accepted way of getting known. Check out the *Writers' and Artists' Yearbook* for their recommendations.

- Before you choose your publisher, seek out recommendations from others who have published using this company.

- You'll pay at least £1,500 (if not much more) if you take this option plus the cost of printing your books. I do remember being quoted £7,500 when I was looking for a publisher for my first book. Not surprisingly, I didn't take them up on this offer!

- Check out Matador (part of the Troubador group) who published my first book via this method. They have published their own guide to self-publishing which is worth a read, and this can be downloaded via their website at www.troubador.co.uk/matador.

How to self-publish your book

The third option is to self-publish your book, and getting your book published in this way is now more accepted by the industry and by readers. Statistics indicate that the UK share of the market for self-published books grew by 79% in 2013, with 18 million self-published books bought by UK readers.

The book industry is worth approximately £59 million, however self-published books only account for a small proportion of the overall market – 5% of the 323 million total books bought, and 3% of the £2,185m spent on books last year (source www.theguardian.co.uk – Nielsen Book).

Many now-successful authors have started this way, such as James Redfield, the author of *The Celestine Prophecy*, which later was acquired by Warner Books and sold over 20 million copies (source *The Huffington Post*).

It is true that deciding to go down the self-publishing route can appear daunting, because you are doing it yourself. However, there are companies that can make this process easy for you. These are some of the advantages and disadvantages of choosing this method and I'll share my experiences shortly.

Advantages

- You retain editorial control over your book, and do not have to conform to the requirements of a publishing house. This means that it is up to you what you write and publish in your book (which may have disadvantages too).

- As with partnership publishing, you are the publisher, so you will also maintain control over the rights of your book, and you can do what you like with your book and the material.

- You can publish your book quickly, which is essential if you are publishing the book to promote at an event.

- It can be relatively cheap to print and distribute your book. Also, you can usually print-on-demand, which reduces upfront costs and the need for finding space to store unsold books.

- It can be easier when you choose a company to take care of the ISBN number, the legal requirements, printing and distribution (otherwise you need to do this yourself).

- You are responsible for setting a price for your book. You also take the profits of book sales when you sell directly (or less a percentage in the region of 40-60% of your book's selling price if you sell via Amazon or other bookstores). So please make sure that you price your book accordingly so that you ideally make some money from your book, or at the very least cover your costs.

- It is easy to get published, although you do still need to produce a great book to retain your credibility.

- If you are lucky, publishing your book in this way may still result in a traditional publisher contacting you later. But if you don't do it, you'll never know!

Disadvantages

- Self-publishing may be seen as less professional than having a traditional publisher.

- It can be time consuming if you don't get the right support.

- There is a cost to making your book look professional. You will need to source your own editor/proofreader, a designer to do your artwork, cover design and typesetting, and a printing company. You need to find someone who will do a good job for you, so getting a recommendation is ideal.

- Unless you employ a company to do it for you, you will need to take account of legal requirements and sourcing an ISBN number (see below).

- You will need to market the book yourself, although there are people who specialise in this area (see the next section).

I published my second book, *How to Stand Out in your Business*, through the self-publishing route. There were a couple of reasons for this, which I will share with you shortly. There are various options in this area, including Completely Novel, who I used for my second book, or www.lulu.com and www.createspace.com (an Amazon company), although I do not have any experience of using either of these options.

Tips for self-publishing

- I'd like to reiterate that it is important not to skimp on the editing process. As the author you will be close to the book, so having another pair of eyes or more is essential. As well as employing an editor, you may wish to ask for feedback from valued contacts or clients.

- You will need to fulfil the legal requirements of publishing your book if you do everything yourself. In the UK, as the publisher, you are obliged to send a copy of your publication to the British Library, free of charge, within a month of the date of publication. You are also required to deposit a copy of your book at five other libraries within the UK during the first year. Full details of these libraries and the requirements can be found here: www.legaldeposit.org.uk. This is a requirement of the Legal Deposit Libraries Act 2003.

- You will also need an ISBN number. This stands for International Standard Book Number and is the "Product identifier used by libraries for ordering, listing and stock control purposes" (Source: International ISBN Agency). Although it is not a legal requirement to have one, if you want to sell your book through major bookshops online or via the high street, this is essential. Anyone can order an ISBN number and they are available in blocks of 10 for £132 (in 2014). Details can be found here: www. isbn.nielsenbook.co.uk.

- In addition, you need to fulfil the requirements of the copyright page. If you are using the services of a typesetter, they will be able to do this for you. At the very minimum, you need to include your own copyright notice and name, the publisher's details (likely to be you if you are self-publishing), the year of first publication of the work and the ISBN number. For up-to-date guidance on this area, you can consult the *Writers' and Artist's Yearbook*.

- You may also be wondering what print-on-demand actually means. Instead of getting hundreds or thousands of books printed, you can print as required. You'll often order one or more books and they will be printed and delivered in a few days.

- Although it can seem expensive to list your book on Amazon and other online bookstores, this does help you to get a wider reach. Also remember that you are unlikely to make money from your book itself; the payback comes from boosting your credibility and reaching more clients. Just remember when you sell your book from your own stock, you do get 100% of the profits!

As someone who has gone down both of these routes, let me share with you my experiences, and feel free to contact me so that I can tell you how I can help you to get your book published.

Case study: Karen Williams, my experiences of publishing two books (prior to this one!)

When I was writing my first book, I spent a lot of time trying to navigate the publishing maze. This actually slowed down my book and was mind-blowing too!

I started by looking for a publishing deal and purchasing the *Writers' and Artists' Yearbook* was my best buy. It helped me to develop a pretty good pitch, understand what the publishing houses wanted, and what made my book different.

However, it was a distraction and there are easier ways of doing it.

Eventually, I decided to go down the partnership publishing route with Matador. They'd been recommended in the *Yearbook* and by a friend of mine who was a PR Consultant. Working in partnership with them was easy. Although I'd already sourced my own editor who also proofread the book, they did everything else in conjunction with me.

The main downside with partnership publishing is that you pay for the privilege of getting published and to make it cost effective, you need to decide how many books to order in advance.

To give you a flavour of the costs, this route cost me just shy of £3,000 which is a fair sum when you have no idea how well your book is going to do, although at the time I didn't realise the advantages of being a published author. However, this fee did include the editing, the publishing services and cover design, 1,000 copies of the book, distribution, Kindle book, and a marketing package.

When I was looking at publishing, I also looked at the traditional publishing route and had contacted a couple of publishers, but didn't hear anything initially. Ironically I was approached by one of the traditional publishers at the same time as I was signing the contract with Matador, but due to the factors highlighted above in terms of the disadvantages of taking this option (I'd done my research by then), I decided to take the partnership publishing route.

By the second time, I felt like I was able to do it myself. I'd spent a lot of time researching the industry for my first book and had started to develop good contacts in this area. Also I had also set myself a deadline of getting my book finished and printed for an event I was running in November 2012, so my timescales were tight. I'd actually planned, written and published this book within six months.

I used the same editor and she recommended an expert to me who could do the typesetting and cover design. Going down the self-publishing route cost me just over £1,000, although this didn't include book printing.

For this book, I chose to use Completely Novel because I could print-on-demand at a realistic subscription of £7.99 per month, which included getting the book onto Amazon and other online bookstores, distribution, as well as supplying an ISBN number. Every time I need some more books to sell personally or give away, all I need to do is order them on the website, and for approximately £3.50-£4 a copy, they are delivered to me in just a few days. I've certainly found this to be an advantage when I use this book to raise my credibility and share my expertise. I uploaded the book to Kindle myself when a colleague of mine showed me how easy it was to do it!

Karen Williams
www.selfdiscoverycoaching.co.uk

Get your book onto Kindle

According to *The Bookseller*, e-Book purchases in the UK rose by 20% in 2013, with self-published titles accounting for one-in-five sales (source Nielsen's Books & Consumers Conference as published on www.thebookseller.com).

Also stated in *The Bookseller*, according to an Ofcom study into digital consumption, it was found that Kindle (owned by Amazon) has a dominant 79% share of the e-Book market in the UK.

Not only will your e-Book appeal to those with a Kindle reader, many smartphones and tablets also allow you to download the Kindle app and read books via this device. If you publish using one of the three methods already identified, you can also publish your book on Kindle, although you could choose Kindle only and offer your book exclusively online.

Using Amazon's Kindle Direct Publishing Platform, you can reach a large audience of prospective readers, and can earn 35% or 70% of royalties depending on the price of your book (correct in 2014).

 Top tip: When using your book as your hook, my opinion is that having both a Kindle and physical book are important. Although some people will want to download your book, I do believe that your book on your prospective client's bookshelf is more likely to encourage them to contact you. It also gives you a physical product to sell or give away at an event. In addition, many people prefer to have a printed copy of a book to thumb through and annotate.

Both of my first two books are available via Kindle and as a printed book, and I'll continue to go down this route with this one.

Tips for Kindle publishing

- If you go down the traditional publishing route, having a Kindle version may be included as part of your package. If you decide to pursue one of the self-publishing options, you may need to do this yourself. When you are seeking support, there are people who will do this for you.

- However, it is surprisingly simple to upload your own Kindle book and there are step-by-step guides available on Kindle, not surprisingly enough!

Lastly, you may also consider, at some stage, having your book available in audio format. Check out ACX (www.acx.com), an Amazon company, where you can create an audio version of your book for distribution through Audible, Amazon and iTunes.

Things to think about

There are various ways to publish your book and whichever option you choose, don't try to do everything yourself.

If you are self-publishing, don't skimp on costs either as your finished book will reflect on your brand.

Don't let your potential publishing efforts distract you from writing and finishing your book.

Be aware that whichever option you choose, you'll be doing the marketing!

Action points to get published

Nail your synopsis as soon as possible to get clear on what you are pitching to a publisher, and how to sell your book.

Do your research when choosing the right publisher or self-publishing, and get recommendations from people who have done it already.

If self-publishing, get prices up front so that you know what it is likely to cost you.

Don't be afraid to do it yourself with support along the way.

To get access to the brilliant blueprint on this section, go to the website www.yourbookisthehook.com/downloads, where you'll also find other relevant information to help you to publish your book.

Section 6
Marketing must-knows

The most important part of creating and writing your book comes after you've finished and published it (although please don't wait until this point to get started with your promotion). Unless you have an effective marketing strategy for your book, your time and energy will be wasted. Is it really worth putting your best stuff in print if nobody reads it and you don't use it to leverage your knowledge and expertise?

As I mentioned in the last chapter, even if you are fortunate enough to get a brilliant publishing deal through an agent or direct with a publishing house, the marketing and promotion of the book will be up to you!

I'd like you to bear in mind that if you've followed my strategies in this book and you're using your book as the hook to get you noticed, then this bit shouldn't be a problem for you. You should already have some of this in place, and be willing to work on any gaps to get your book in front of your prospective clients.

By using a range of online and offline tools, your book will get you noticed and help you to reach the clients who want to know your stuff, many of whom may well want to work with you on a personal level.

In the following chapters, I'm going to be sharing with you the must-know strategies for marketing and promoting your book. Although there may be a few things that you know already, others are synonymous with writing and publishing a book, so you need to be willing to explore the ideas and put some of them into place. Many of these will help you to create a buzz with your book – and need to be in place even before you've finished it! Other options will be more relevant later like getting your book to number one on Amazon, arranging a book launch to start your promotion with a bang, and PR strategies that will complement your book.

But before I do that, let's get started with the marketing basics to get your book noticed online. These are things that you may be doing already, but are you using these effectively? I'll be sharing some of the best strategies that I normally reserve for my one-to-one clients, so without further ado... read on.

Chapter 14
Online strategies to
market your book

If you've ever wondered how to promote and market your book, whilst making the most of what you have already, and perhaps by adding a few simple tools to your toolkit, then don't miss out on this chapter! Here are some of the approaches you need to take as a published author to get your book noticed.

Many of these strategies interlink so take a look through all of the ideas, as you'll need a combination of these online strategies with offline tactics to help promote your book.

Develop a website for your book

If you are religiously following my suggestions in this book, I assume you already have a business website that promotes you and your business. You'll also have a system in place to generate leads, and you'll be keeping in touch with your community regularly. You'll also have a message, and product and sales funnels that support your book. If you haven't done this already, then this is the essential place to start. The purpose of your business website isn't to just have an online presence; it is about helping your prospects to make an informed decision about whether you can help them, and then helping them to buy from you (see more about this in section 1).

For your book, though, you might consider getting a new website solely to promote it. Or at the very least, make sure you have a page for it on your existing website and drive traffic to it. However, it is pretty simple to create a one page squeeze page (otherwise known as a lead page or sales page) just for your book. A great tool to use for this is the Squeeze Page Toolkit (www.squeezepagetoolkit.com), which uses a drag and drop system to allow you to add different types of content to the page, including headlines, images, links (to your book!), and perhaps a video if you choose to use this medium (it is a great way to stand out!).

 Top tip: Buy the web address for your book as soon as you've decided the title, so you don't miss out on this promotion opportunity. There are plenty of online providers who will enable you to buy the domain for around £5-£10 per year.

You can launch your website before your book is published. You want to create a buzz about your book, and what better motivator to get your book finished than to tell people you are writing it!

If you want to tell people about your book now and use this to grow your list, read these tips from Dan Harrison to help you to get off the starting blocks.

How to use a list to get sales for your book – Dan Harrison shares five tips to sell your book before it's even published

Ok, so you're super-focused on writing your book. How would you like to build some customers for your book? Creating your book is half of the challenge; you'll clearly want customers to buy your book too. A great way to do this is with a pre-launch list.

Lists are extremely valuable in any business, as you can invest time in building a small database of contacts who are specifically interested in what you offer, and then focus your attention on those contacts to make your sales. The result is that sales are easier, and you don't have to do any 'hard sells'.

You can use a very similar principle to help sell your book. In five steps, I'll explain how you can do this yourself before you've even finished your book!

1. Create a simple web page (called a squeeze page) that collects the name and email address of the visitor. The web page is very simple; it has a picture of your book cover, a short summary of your book, and a list of 3-5 reasons why someone will enjoy reading your book.

2. Offer a free chapter – you could offer a free snippet from your book that you've already

completed, even if it's an early draft. You'd offer this as a PDF file, which the visitor can download or receive via email once they've entered their details. This gives your visitor a taste of your upcoming book.

3. Connect the web page to an email system such as ActiveCampaign, AWeber or MailChimp. That will make it easy for you to send email updates to the visitors who have signed up. You can give them more snippets and updates on the launch date.

4. Promote the new web page on your social media profiles (so Twitter, Facebook and LinkedIn). You'll start building a list of people who are interested. You could even experiment with Facebook Advertising to target people who like books similar in style to yours. This is the bit that will help motivate you to finish your book, as you'll get more and more people wanting to buy your book!

5. When you're ready to sell, offer your list a special offer. Perhaps they can buy a signed copy of your book directly from you, and get an electronic version for free. Keep it low tech; you might just use PayPal for the money bit. You'll get sales on day one, which is very exciting!

Doing this is not very difficult if you use the right tool. Pop over to www.buildyourlist.co.uk/karen and get detailed instructions on how to do this for your book!

These tips come from Dan Harrison, a specialist in helping businesses grow by helping them to craft lists of their future customers.

Email: dan@squeezepagetoolkit.com
Web: www.squeezepagetoolkit.com

When writing a web page for your book, your completed synopsis may help you, as you'll have already thought about how to pitch your book.

You want to wow your readers with effective headlines, punchy language and persuasive copy. Also you can share what your reviewers think about your book. This is great social proof that demonstrates even more credibility than you can by yourself.

Most importantly you need to tell people how to buy your book! Make sure you link to your Amazon page, an online booking form (if you are managing the distribution yourself), or your preferred way of selling your book.

If you are using a squeeze page to promote your book, make sure that you also tell people who you are and why you are the best person to write this book. You may wish to link to your 'about you' page on your website, so people can get to know you. Just make sure that you don't distract your audience from the purpose of this page, which is, of course, to buy your book.

On your main website, you may also want to include

a media page so that you can easily respond to media requests about your book. Include a press release, cover image of your book, and any other images such as your professional photo that may be used to promote your book.

Create your social media presence

If you are already running a successful business, I assume that you already have an effective social media presence. You'll be on all of the main social media platforms, and sharing valuable content on your Facebook business page, through your LinkedIn profile, and be tweeting a couple of times a day.

You'll be sharing valuable information with your followers and you'll have strategies to build your online communities. You may also have accounts on Pinterest, Instagram, Google+, YouTube, or other social media sites, and be interacting with people on a regular basis.

 **Top tip:** If you decide to approach a traditional publishing house, having a high number of likes on your Facebook page and a large following on Twitter is likely to be essential before they even consider publishing your manuscript.

If you don't yet have a social media presence, then do this now! It's really simple to set up your accounts, it won't cost you a penny, and it's easy to start sharing your message.

If you do have a social media presence, just like with your website, you need to be consistent with your message. Start to share information about your book before you've finished it and be strategic with the content that you are communicating.

One thing that I suggest that all my clients do is create an editorial calendar. This is simply an Excel spreadsheet where you create separate tabs for the updates that you wish to share on social media. For example, if you have a free e-Book or other lead magnet, you could create 10-12 status updates that you can schedule on your social media platforms encouraging people to sign up to your freebie. This could be the title of one of the tabs.

For another tab on the spreadsheet, you may develop a database of useful tips that would appeal to your target client or reader. My top piece of advice is to keep these tips around 120 characters long, then when you share them on Twitter they are easy for your readers to retweet to their followers without losing content.

You could also have a tab for your blog posts. Whenever I write a new blog post I write 5-7 updates (again no more than 120 characters long) that create intrigue, ask a question or encourage my followers to read and comment on my blog posts. This also enables me to repurpose past blog posts rather than write an article once and never do anything with the content again.

You can have as many tabs as you like in your spreadsheet, and you may also include things like inspiring quotes. And of course, you'll want to have one for your book! Why not share quotes direct from your book, endorsements, reviews, and tell people how to buy it.

As well as giving you great resource, your editorial calendar is a time saving tool. You can schedule your posts in advance by using a tool such as Hootsuite, which means that you don't have to be online everyday building your presence, although real time interaction in conjunction with this is good practice.

With all of your social media accounts, make sure you add details of your book too. You may wish to update your description or keywords to include 'Author of...' in the title. Remember also to keep all of the information current and produce material that your community enjoy and want to share.

Start blogging

I'd like to assume that you have a blog already. I'd like to think that you will commit to writing a blog post a couple of times a month, and people love what you have to say. I'd like to imagine that you are getting regular comments, shares and clients from your writing already.

If you don't have a blog, talk to your web designer about adding this feature to your website, as, for natural writers, it is an easy way to share your content with your tribe.

The other way in which you can blog is by being a guest blogger for someone who has their own blog in a complementary area. This is unlikely to be your direct competition but may be someone who shares your target readership. For example, if I was blogging about this book, I'd be seeking to write a guest blog for fellow business coaches who don't specialise in the book process. There may also be specialist bloggers in your genre who are on the lookout for new content, and don't always want to do it themselves – so you will be helping them out! If you do this, make sure that you include a strong biography and photo, plus tell people how they can connect with you and buy your book.

My most important note in this area is to make sure you always add the right keywords or tags to your blog to get them found on the web. You may also use a SEO (Search Engine Optimisation) tool to facilitate this process. Also share your blogs on social media, as I mentioned in the last section, and always repurpose your content. What I mean by this is take sections out of your book, turn blog posts into video content or podcasts, or create an Ezine or printed article. Being found online is essential to reaching new prospects, so please don't miss out on optimising your posts.

For more tips on marketing your business, check out my membership club which has great resources in this subject: www.thebusinesswowfactor.com. There are interviews, blueprints and great tips on areas such as SEO, blogging, list building, creating podcasts, PR, and much more.

How to make best use of Amazon

If your book is going to be on Amazon (which I certainly recommend), make the most of their author tools. Firstly, you need to make sure that your book is presented correctly. This means that it is in the right category, with promotional copy that stands out, and a clear and articulate author biography.

You also want your readers to share their reviews on Amazon. You want as many people as possible to give a star-rating to your book, share their thoughts, and – ideally – give you a positive endorsement.

Amazon also allows you to have your own 'Author page' on their Author Central platform, so make full use of this. Your author page will allow you to share a comprehensive biography, and videos and photographs that may be relevant to you and your business. You can also link to Twitter so it will show your recent tweets (potentially increasing your followers), links to the book(s) you have published which are available on Amazon, events you have planned, and relevant discussions. This is a great platform to engage with potential readers and share useful content and promotions. It also links directly from your book sales page.

Another place you may wish to investigate is Goodreads – www.goodreads.com. Goodreads is an online website that allows the general public to review books, share their thoughts, and rate the books that they have read. As an author, you can set up your book, get new fans, allow people to ask you questions and view statistics on your page.

Top tip: Goodreads also allows you to give away copies of your book, which is a brilliant way to promote it as they'll share the offer with their subscribers.

Things to think about

You can start your online marketing strategy at any time, even before you've started writing your book.

Choose the right tools that work for you and your readers, bearing in mind that regular contact is essential to build effective relationships.

If any of these suggestions feel too difficult, get support to help you to set up your website, social media or get you started with blogging.

To get a special offer on joining The Business Wow Factor, please go to the downloads page: www.yourbookisthehook.com/downloads

Chapter 15
Offline strategies to get
your book noticed

When you are marketing your book, you need to combine your online approach with other strategies if you want to get you and your book noticed. In this chapter, I'll explore how you can make these happen, and I'll start with my favourite method.

How to get speaking engagements

In my second book, *How to Stand out in your Business*, I wrote a whole chapter about getting speaking engagements, and how to get the best results with this medium. Briefly here, I must say that speaking has been one of the best strategies I've used to promote my business and my book.

One of the advantages of being a published author is that your credibility will precede you, even before you decide to speak. Whether you add this to your biography and website, or you use this to engage with the organisers, don't forget to mention it! You'll also find that many people will purchase your book before you speak, and take time to get to know you before you even present your talk.

It goes without saying (but I'll do it anyway!) that you need to speak about a topic related to your book. For example, if your book teaches your signature system, talk in depth about one of the areas, and tell people how they can get access to the other parts through your book or working with you personally.

It should also go without saying that you want to get in front of your ideal clients and readers through your speaking. Start by approaching people who are able to help you to reach these people and offer opportunities for you to share your message. It's also useful to create a speaker profile that you can provide to organisers of such events. This would normally be a one page document that includes a headline for your talk, some of the key points that an audience will get from your talk, plus a short biography. You also may wish to include testimonials from other people who have asked you to speak at their events.

When you've secured the speaking engagement, and you've nailed your content, here are some ideas of how you can use speaking to promote your book:

- You could seek permission to sell your book at the event, and then sell a signed copy at the back of the room after your talk. You may consider offering it at a discounted price to encourage people to buy it there and then.

- You'll find that not everyone present will buy a copy of your book or may have one already. Also when you sell your book, you probably won't automatically get the contact details of audience. So do this! A simple sheet that allows people to complete their name and email address in exchange for something free, like your lead magnet, could work. Then remember to add them to your list – but only with their permission.

- You don't necessarily have to sell your book; you could give it away. You could do a prize draw where everyone in the room gives you their business card and you pick one out randomly. Or you could just simply give a copy to everyone attending. Although it will cost you a small amount of money in printing costs, if you are using your book to get more clients, what better way to get into the minds of people who may want to engage your services on a one-to-one basis? Remember that your book is the hook that gets you noticed, then it's up to you to use this to grow your business further.

You'll also probably find that, just by writing your book, you're more likely to be invited to be a speaker. Actually one of the biggest things I've found since writing my books is that instead of always seeking out opportunities, many come to me just because I am an author. Let me share with you Helen's story, how her book was developed, and how it helped her business.

Case study: Helen Lindop, co-author of *Start a Family Friendly Business: 129 Brilliant Business Ideas For Mums* with Antonia Chitty

Start a Family Friendly Business was published in September 2010 and grew out of my blog, BusinessPlusBaby.com.

I started Business Plus Baby because my career wasn't flexible enough for me as a mum to a new baby. I needed to know which businesses *would* work around a baby so started to research business ideas, but I couldn't find a list of family-friendly businesses anywhere. I spent hours trawling the internet, on Twitter and on Facebook, plus I went along to the first 'Mum's The Boss' networking meetings to find out what other business mums were doing.

A few months later I'd seriously considered at least six business ideas and none were right for me, but I thought that they might help someone else. So I wrote a series of blog posts called 'Business Ideas For Mums', giving the pros and cons of each idea. I thought that I might use these as a starting point for an e-Book eventually, but I hadn't bargained on the magic of blogging!

Antonia Chitty and I 'met' through our blogs; hers is FamilyFriendlyWorking.co.uk. By coincidence Antonia had been thinking of writing a book of business ideas just like mine, so we joined forces and together we wrote *Start a Family Friendly Business*. We realised that you need more than just a good idea though, so we included step-by-step guides on how to choose your business idea and how to check that it'll work for you.

Promoting the book – especially with my name next to Antonia's, who was already an established author and blogger for business mums –

definitely helped raise my profile. I'm sure it was a factor in me being invited to speak at the 'Cambridge Business Mums' Conference' in 2011 and the 'Britmums Parent Blogger Conference' in 2013. It had a huge impact on my confidence, too. Having my children and leaving my career definitely affected my confidence and writing this book, getting it published, and hearing from people who actually read it, was a huge boost for me. Especially as I was completely shattered and spent most of my time feeding babies and changing nappies!

Looking back, I can see that having a book published is an incredible launch pad for other opportunities but that often, you need to create those for yourself. For example, if you're a newcomer as I was, the chances are you'd need to network with people who could give you speaking opportunities rather than just waiting to be asked. As a mum to children aged just one and two years when the book was published, my ability to make and grab these opportunities was quite limited. Had I written that book now they are at school it would have been a different story!

Helen Lindop
www.businessplusbaby.com

Develop your media contacts

I'll be talking more about PR in the next section, although I'd like to touch on it here briefly. I've already mentioned that having a media pack available to download from your website is essential, but you also need to be proactive about getting media coverage. It's unlikely you're just going to be found without doing any legwork first. The best way of getting into the media is by employing a specialist to help you, but if you decide to do it yourself, here are a few tips.

- Create a 'media list' of magazines, papers, or other publications which reach your target readers. Get to know the editors and writers, bearing in mind that some journalists will work for multiple publications. Then why don't you contact them? Your media list may include unusual publications which are favoured by your ideal reader.

- When you do contact journalists, remember that it's not all about your book or you; they are always looking for a juicy story. So you'll probably be selling the reason why you wrote the book, the turning point that prompted you to get your thoughts on paper, or any other relevant story that might (again) be a hook.

- You'll also find that some of the specialist magazines (both physical and online) may be willing to review your book and publish this in their magazine. They may also be willing to include an article submission, an extract from the book, or interview you for the publication.

- Having a pre-prepared press release will help you in this area. Some publishers may do this for you, especially if you've published through the traditional or partnership routes. A good press release will include the key selling points, and a brief summary of your book, covering image, author information and your photo. Plus it should include how people can order your book. Please see the next chapter for further tips in this area.

In July 2014, I was featured in an article in The *Daily Express* newspaper. This happened because my PR Consultant saw a request on Twitter seeking people with unusual stories to tell, and she told me about this opportunity. When I talked to the journalist, she was very interested in my upcoming book *The Mouse that Roared* and my own story about the 'Year to Live' project that I undertook in 2012. This ultimately led to an interview, photo shoot and a two page article in the newspaper.

 Top tip: #journorequest is the Twitter tag that you need to watch!

What you may also find, though, is that you'll have to do much less work to get PR. Sometimes you just need to be in the right place at the right time, so let me tell you about what happened to Mary.

Case study: Mary Waring, author of *The Wealthy Woman: A Man is Not a Financial Plan*

I published my book in January 2014. The date was specifically chosen – firstly to coincide with New Year resolutions to take more control of finances, and secondly to appeal to women going through divorce, which often spikes in January.

By a marvellous piece of luck, by being in the right place at the right time, I managed to get a full page article in the *Daily Mail* on 2 January. I couldn't have chosen a better paper, since my ideal client will often be a *Daily Mail* reader. From this I had an article in the *Daily Express*, several BBC radio stations, and a number of online blogs. As a result, advance orders starting pouring in.

The book had initially been written with a view to handing out to clients, potential clients and professional connections. I hadn't anticipated actually making money from it: it was designed to be part of my marketing kit. However, receiving 1,800 advance orders from Amazon changed all that.

The book has made a very healthy profit and has obtained significant PR for me and my business. Even now, 10 months later, I still get calls from potential clients who tell me they found me in the *Daily Mail* article. I've had one potential client who initially found me from the PR articles and then purchased a copy of my book. She has now contacted me to arrange a meeting. She is extremely wealthy with assets of £40 million. Now, who knows if she will end up being a client, but I'm not sure that lady would have found me had the book not been there generating publicity.

Being an author marks me out as an authority in my field, and allows me to stand out as different to my competitors. It doesn't mean I'm better than them or that I necessary provide a better service, but it all helps to provide me with a higher profile than the majority of people in my industry.

Due to a number of changes in the financial services industry this year I am considering updating the book. The original plan had been to direct readers to my website where there is a page providing updates. However, due to the success of the book in helping me build my brand and generate some fantastic publicity, I will probably release a revised edition so I can obtain some fresh PR.

If you're considering writing a book, my advice is DO IT. It will help you gain expert status and as part of a marketing and PR plan can hopefully significantly advance your business.

Mary Waring
www.wealth-for-women.co.uk

Hold a virtual or physical event

When promoting your book, you may wish to do a book signing in a local bookshop. This will usually be organised direct with the bookstore, and it can be a good opportunity to meet potential readers. Although this will only work for some books, and may not be the right option for you.

So what's stopping you doing a virtual event? If you are aiming to hit the number one spot on Amazon (see the next chapter), then this will certainly be part of your marketing strategy. However, you don't need to organise your own event; you could arrange to get interviewed on the radio (this may be local, national or blog-talk radio), or ask your contacts to interview you about your book and then share with their community.

Other ideas to consider

If that's not enough to whet your appetite, here are a few other ideas to consider:

- Always carry a copy of your book around with you, especially if you are attending networking or other business events. You never know who may want to get their hands on a copy, and it is a good positioning tool.

- Remember to introduce yourself as a published author as part of your elevator pitch, as it gives credibility to what you stand for. You can use your book as a prop too.

- You may also wish to exhibit at events if this is relevant to your business. This is also an ideal opportunity to approach the organiser to speak at this event as well as having a stand for people to visit and meet you. If you'd prefer not to exhibit, then you could always attend the event and speak to other people who are promoting their services who may be interested in your expertise.

- Business success is about building relationships, so who do you know (or need to know) with whom you can share the message about your book? What can you do for them in return?

- Tell everyone you know about your book. Although I didn't mention it explicitly earlier, make sure you tell people who are already in your community through your newsletter and other mediums such as your personal and business Facebook page and groups to which you belong.

- Send copies of your books to prominent people in your industry and ask them to endorse your book, even after it has been published. This could be a great opportunity to get your book onto the reading list of university courses, recommended to students, etc, depending on the content of course!

- Get an app for your book. Physically distributing your book is great, but an app is a brilliant way of sharing the content with your audience and adding even more value. A good app will enable you to continue to engage with your subscribers, add new content and extra value, and send push notifications with additional support, resources, and encouragement, or events and workshops that you are running.

- Write your next book. "What?" I hear you say... "I haven't finished the first one yet!" However, a great way to get known for what you do is to write multiple books on your topic(s) of expertise. You may write the first book on your signature system generally, and book number two could be going more deeply into your favourite strategy; a little bit like this one! Then book number three could be taking part of this content and going even deeper into one of the sub-categories. For example, I could write a book just on book PR and marketing if I wished to do this.

- Within your professional area, what else could you do? Write a list on the page now... What other ideas could you pursue?

Things to think about

However you publish your book, you are in charge of promoting and marketing your book.

If you are already established as a business owner, some of these strategies are likely to be in place in your business.

There are many tools that you can choose to promote your book. Choose the mediums that work for you, bearing in mind that some interlink with each other.

Using one of the principles of persuasion, other people praising and promoting your book will help you to reach a wider audience and attract new followers.

Chapter 16
Three ways to create a
buzz with your book

In the last chapters, I've shared various basic strategies that you can do to get your book noticed, and in this section, I'd like to share with you three other things that you can do to create a buzz about your book.

How to get to number one on Amazon

Getting to number one on Amazon is one of the strategies you may choose to adopt. It is great to be able to say that you are an Amazon bestselling author in your publicity, on your website and in future books.

When I launched my first book, I learnt how to get to number one on Amazon. I adapted the process that I learnt from my mentors and carried it out for myself. It worked. My book reached number one in my overall category of Business, Finance and Law (overtaking such classics as *Influence: The Psychology of Persuasion* by Robert Cialdini and *Think and Grow Rich* by Napoleon Hill) and number 248 overall on Amazon, competing with thousands of other book titles across all genres.

I followed a similar strategy with my second book, but I didn't reach those dizzy heights of number one status with this book, for various reasons which I'll share here.

There are various variations of this plan employed by authors and publishers, and this is my interpretation in an easy to follow and simple way.

1. Decide your launch day

Decide what day you wish to launch your book and designate this as your launch day. You'll probably want to choose a weekday, depending on your book and the audience you are looking to attract. What you want to do is to encourage everybody you know to buy a copy of your book on this specific day to (hopefully) propel it to the top of the charts.

2. Create an offer for your launch day

For your book launch, why don't you make it a no-brainer and offer bonuses to incentivise people to buy your book on that specific day? Create a webpage for your offer, and give people the benefits of your offer, and how it will help them.

For example, you could run a webinar that complements your book, which is only available for people who buy on that day. Or you could offer another bonus, for example a one-to-one call for the first x number of people who buy a copy, or another product that supports your launch.

I've seen other people adapt this process by having other business owners offer their products too. But I believe that this can make the offer overwhelming and difficult to manage, which I'm seeking to avoid here.

3. Ask for 'helpers' in your community to promote your book on this launch day

For both of my online launches, I created a list of people aka 'helpers' or joint venture partners who I contacted to support me. As I had interviewed many coaches for my first book, this was automatically my first port of call for book one, and many of them sent the information to their list – which was one of the secrets behind my success when I promoted this book. My list of helpers was pretty long – 50-100 people from recollection, and the more people, the better, as long as they have a strong community of people who are likely to be your potential readers, of course.

To do this, I developed a standard email which I personally sent to everyone on my list of helpers. The email told people what I was doing, a brief synopsis of the book, my plan for the launch and the date I'd planned, and a date by which I would like them to reply. With my first book, I directed my helpers to a page on my website that had a sign-up box to make it easy for people to say 'yes' to helping me. I asked them to share the numbers of people on their list and it had tick boxes so that they could indicate how they were willing to share my launch, i.e. via their newsletter, Twitter, Facebook, etc.

Top tip: You will need to plan your launch many weeks, if not months, in advance if you want some of the big names in your profession to promote your book for you. I didn't have a long lead-in time for my second book, which thwarted my Amazon quest!

4. Get ready for your launch

You will need to set up a web page for your launch day. This will include details about your book, any supporting offers, and ultimately this is the sales page to get people to buy your book on this day. Make sure that you include a link to your Amazon page and a way for people to get a copy of the bonuses. Ideally have a sign-up box where your new reader has to leave their name, email address, and Amazon order number. They will also automatically join your mailing list so that you can follow up with them.

5. Help your helpers!

When I carried out my online launches, I created a list of everyone who had said yes and then I made it easy for them to promote me. I designed emails for them to send out to their communities. I wrote Facebook and Twitter updates so that they could share the information (that I wanted them to share). I also gave them the choice to amend these materials to suit their audience, which was especially applicable for the standard email. I asked them to direct their followers to the page I mentioned in the fourth point.

I reminded my helpers the day before the launch, on the launch day itself and also thanked them for their help afterwards.

6. Promote it yourself

As well as asking your helpers to promote your offer, it is also essential that you do it yourself through your newsletter, social media and any other opportunities you have during this day. These other opportunities may be forums in which you are involved, other communities, LinkedIn groups and the like. You could run a series of targeted Facebook or Google advertisements alongside this. You could also engage in relevant online conversations or physical conversations too.

7. Measure your success and follow up

You can measure your success by taking screenshots of your progress on Amazon as the day progresses, and you'll be able to compare your ranking at different times.

You ideally also need to create autoresponders to follow up with new readers who buy your book. When I did this, I included the bonuses and also a follow-up sequence to tell my readers how else I could help them. Then remember to ask your new readers to leave an Amazon review!

This plan will help you to create a buzz with the book. It is not designed as a long term strategy to keep you at the top of Amazon, as this only works with a more comprehensive marketing plan in conjunction with this process. But it is designed to help you to create a buzz for the book, reach more people than you can do alone, and (ideally) reach the top of the charts!

For personal support to develop a bespoke strategy for getting to number one on Amazon, email karen@selfdiscoverycoaching.co.uk to organise a chat.

Get noticed with a book launch party

There's nothing like a deadline to give you a kick up the backside to finish your book (as I've said already), and having a book launch party is one of them.

I held events for both of my first two books and I've been to a few book launches too. Just like having an Amazon launch, having a party will create a buzz for your book. It's a great excuse for contacting friends, business contacts and clients and asking them to join you.

Whether you charge for the event or offer it for free, it's also a great place to (again) demonstrate your credibility and share your knowledge. If you've run events before, then follow the strategies that you'd normally use, and here are some strategies that I can briefly share.

For my first book launch, I invited everyone I knew to the event. Of course, these were mainly business contacts and people close to me with whom I wanted to celebrate the occasion. As it was my first book, it was a very special celebration and I also invited the people I'd interviewed – a couple of whom travelled hundreds of miles to be there.

I held the event at a lovely hotel and booked their biggest room. This was just as well as over 70 people turned up for the book launch!

I used the event as an opportunity to share my

story, my experiences and why I'd written the book. It was another chance to demonstrate why my book was different and what people would get from reading it. Although I didn't charge for people to attend, I sold my book through the event, and told people what was coming up next. I also asked my mentor and two of my friends to do a short talk – and they were better than me at praising my book and my expertise!

I also used it as a PR opportunity and contacted my local paper. I had a photographer present, which helped me to make an impact online too. Directly before the event I was also interviewed on Portsmouth Live TV and this was a great chance to promote my book and my business.

The hotel offered me a discount, as although I provided tea and coffee – and branded cupcakes – there was a cash bar too. This also encouraged attendees to network and build relationships with each other.

I also carried out a charity raffle. I asked many of my business friends to donate books that they had written to raise money for my chosen charity.

For my second book, I was holding my first Star Biz conference and I purposely completed it to launch at this event. Although this was a fairly low key affair, having a date in mind certainly gets you focused.

These are my suggestions to organise your successful book launch.

1. Decide on a date, time and a venue that will represent your brand. Ideally a venue that is easily accessible by car and train is best.

2. Choose whether to charge for entry or offer the event for free. Another option would be to charge for the event and include a copy of your book as part of the entrance fee, or include a charity donation in the ticket price too. I've seen all of these options work.

3. Write a list of everyone you'd like to attend and invite them. Setting up an event page on your website or using a tool like Eventbrite (www.eventbrite.com) will make it easier to manage your event.

4. Prepare a short talk and structure for the event. For example, you may wish to share your story, tell some anecdotes from the book, or even hold a mini-workshop to demonstrate your expertise.

5. You may also invite other people to be part of the event and do a short talk or teach something relevant to your book and its content. As much as you may not like it, though, remember that you are the star of the show!

6. Sell your book at the event and use it as an opportunity to tell people what you are doing next, and perhaps have a special promotion for attendees when they book at the launch party.

7. Have a support team of people helping you as you don't want to be the person doing everything when you are the person in the spotlight!

8. When people arrive, have someone welcome people at the door and outline the plan for the evening. This person may also direct people to the bar, your signing table or any other facilities that you've arranged. Also having an official book signing will help you to promote your book and your programmes.

9. Get someone to photograph or video the event for you, so that you can share it with people who couldn't make it, and use it as a great PR opportunity.

10. Talking about PR, make sure you make the most of the occasion. Contact your local paper, TV station and radio. And remember it's all about the story rather than your book launch.

11. Enjoy the day or evening, and have fun! Remember that this is your time to shine, so even if you're an introvert like me, savour every moment.

Create a perfect press release

Another great way to create a buzz for your book is to get your story into the national or local press.

Here are some great tips from Helen Best from Booked PR.

The perfect press release
– Helen Best shows you how to write the perfect press release

No matter how great your book is, if people don't know about it, it will never sell. The press release is a vital tool in your publicity campaign which helps you tell the world that your new book is available for purchase. It's often emailed or posted to the media with a review copy of the book. An effective press release is written in a journalistic format that mimics how a magazine or newspaper would write about your book.

Remember, you are not targeting a bookshop buyer (that's the job of the Advance Information sheet, which is usually compiled by your publisher or sales team – if you have one). Because the press release is such an important part of your media pack and as there is a trend among inexperienced publicists to turn the announcement into an advertisement that journalists will reject, not embrace, it's important to understand how to write a press release that will get read and used. Here are ten of my best tips designed to help you avoid common and costly errors.

Use the traditional news release format

This includes a headline, release date, your announcement written in a journalistic style, publication details (including ISBN, publisher, price and stockists), author biography, author website address, author photograph, the book's cover image and your (or your publicist's) contact details. If the book has received any pre-publication praise, include this too.

Remember that you are not the news

Your book is the news. Unless your name is recognisable, don't use it in the headline. 'World War II secrets uncovered' is more compelling than 'John Brown's first book about World War II'. Although your book is the news, a new book being published is not news – it happens each and every day! Your press release headline needs to be punchy and highlight the book's USP (unique selling point). Take your ego out of it. Take your natural inclination to sell, sell, sell out of it. Look at your story with a cold, objective eye.

First impressions count

An eye-catching headline is crucial. Remember, the journalist isn't interested in how many books you want to sell; they just want a good story to fill editorial space. Write a dynamic first paragraph that is designed to hook your reader's attention. Space permitting, try to include some brief information about the book or chapter titles.

Insert quote here

Including quotes from a reliable source can be an important addition to your press release. Quotes help to prove credibility, give perspective, can add a 'human touch' to the release and, if the release is used verbatim, that's the quote the journalist will use in their story. Include a good quote from you, a reader, or a supporting expert. However, ensure that the quote is not just self-promotional bumph that turns off a journalist. Make it authentic and interesting, maybe adding more detail to the story in your own words.

Keep it short

Organise your thoughts into three or four paragraphs. The entire press release must fit on a single page; otherwise you're likely to lose interest before the book has even been opened. This also makes it neat and easy to read when enclosing a copy with each review copy you mail out.

Think about the format

I've worked as a busy journalist and know for a fact that sometimes attachments get overlooked, so if you are choosing to use email to send out your press release then it's worth including a brief pitch in the body of the email itself, as this may be the only text that is read. Also, consider producing the press release in a format that is widely accessible. Perhaps Microsoft Word, or convert the press release to PDF to produce a snazzy, eye-catching page which is easy to forward on or print. However, remember that clicking on the attachment takes effort and it's easier for a journalist to scan the contents of an email that's already open.

Be creative

If you're sending the press release by post then why not be creative? I've heard of authors including a chocolate bar with their review copies so that the book reviewer can take some time out to read their book. Last year I used black envelopes when promoting a book on the predicted 'end of the world' to attract the attention of journalists. I think the fact that my author soon after appeared on *Sky News* and was invited to write for the UK's biggest selling newspaper was no coincidence!

Spell check

Always check the text several times for typos and grammatical mistakes as these distract the journalist's focus from your story and make you look unprofessional (especially as an author!). Don't just use a computer spell-checker, it's best to also print it out and read through again. Once you're happy there are no mistakes, ask someone else to check – it's amazing what a second pair of eyes can spot.

Hit send!

Distribute your press release with a covering email that briefly highlights the main points and tells the journalist exactly why this book is of interest and how they could feature it. Make life easy for the journalist; the more you make somebody work to use your information, the less likely they are to do so. In addition to distributing your release to your targeted media outlets, post the release on your website so it can be found by search engine users. It's also worth researching appropriate news wire services; there are lots of free services online.

Catch your coverage

As well as monitoring the media you approach, it's also worth signing up to Google Alerts and perhaps consider subscribing to a press clippings agency. You will most likely miss some of the media coverage – or come across it late – but you should be able to track the 'big' media mentions by monitoring your Amazon sales ranking. It's great when you see the correlation between publicity and sales; it makes all of the hard work worth it. Remember, even if you don't get media coverage first time around, you've brought your name to the attention of the journalists who are important to you to enable you to start forming a positive working relationship.

Helen Best and her team at Booked PR offer press release consultations for authors.

Email: helen@bookedpr.com
Web: www.bookedpr.com

Things to think about

Planning your book launch and marketing is essential. Don't just wait for things to happen; you need to consider this from the start.

Get support from other people to get your book out to more people than you can reach alone.

Choose the right strategies depending on your audience and your book.

You don't have to wait until your book is published to tell people about it!

Action points to market your book

Develop a plan for your book launch and ongoing marketing. There are simple strategies that you can put into place now that will make a big difference to getting you and your book noticed.

Get marketing support in areas where you don't excel.

Always consider how you can use your book to elevate your status and expertise, and remember that it is your hook to growing your business and attracting more clients.

For more ideas, strategies and thoughts about marketing your book, and to access the visual blueprint that accompanies this section, go to www.yourbookisthehook.com/downloads

Chapter 17
How to get business
from your book

Well congratulations! Once you've taken all the steps in this book, you'll be the proud author of a book that will help you to grow your business. You'll find that it will become the hook that gets you noticed, that allows you to have a wider reach and attract more clients, and it will be the catalyst to take your business to the next level.

In this final chapter, I want to make sure that you make the most of what you've written, rather than leaving it on a shelf gathering dust.

- What are the next steps for your business?

- How are you going to use your book to get you noticed?

- What's your long term strategy for your business and your book?

Writing a book will help you in the long term and I'd like to remind you that it's a marathon not a sprint! There are ways that you can strategically use your book (or your books!) to grow your business, and I'll share some of these now. Although I have inferred some of these throughout the book, here are a few additional thoughts to consider.

Get leads by giving away your book

Are there particular people you know who can help your business? If so, take some copies of your book and put them in the post.

For example, this may be potential corporate clients who don't yet know you exist, but you'd like to get in through the front door rather than battle with the gatekeeper when you phone up to speak to them. This is a brilliant way to set you aside from your competitors, as it is memorable. A good book won't go in the bin like a letter or flyer might, and won't be deleted like an email.

You could also send a copy to influential people in your field who may be willing to support you and your book. For example, after I published my second book, I sent a copy to someone who runs a coach training school in the UK. I inadvertently attracted a new client because he was singing my praises at an event he was running. Although this client was already on my email list, this was the catalyst that persuaded her that she needed to work with me.

Giving away your book as a gift is also a great strategy when you want to get a potential prospect interested in what you have to say and your message. This may be someone who has expressed an interest in what you are doing, but they are not ready to commit to working with you. A surprise gift will not only endear you to them, but will educate them in the way in which you can help them too.

You could also give away your book to anyone who subscribes to your lead magnet or run a special offer. What a great next step to give to your subscribers! Ultimately isn't it worth spending a few pounds to potentially reach more people who may wish to work with you?

Here's a brilliant case study to inspire you if you would like to employ this strategy.

Case study: Wendy Shand, Tots to Travel and author of *Empty Weeks? How To Get More Bookings And Make Money From Your Holiday Home*

My first piece of advice when it comes to writing a book is to decide what the function of the book is in the first place. Is it autobiographical or is it a lead generating tool? The latter is the reason why I wrote my first book. I was in a mentoring group at the time, and writing a book was seen as a good way of positioning yourself in your marketplace.

At Tots to Travel, we work with families and property owners, and I needed a seesaw to generate leads on both sides. The greatest success in our business is achieved by recruiting the right property owners. I knew what our customers wanted when they went on holiday, but found that property owners didn't necessarily see it in the same way. I wanted to use the book to re-educate owners, and I was prepared to be disruptive and brave in my message.

For me, writing a book was a no-brainer, and I now know that what I was doing was becoming a thought leader in our industry. I had all of this information in my head that I knew owners found interesting. I also knew that I needed to get it out to them, and I also wanted to build our database. In just a couple of weeks I got stuck in and wrote my book and sent it off to an editor, then engaged a local printer to get the copies printed.

I launched the book and it was immediately picked up by the *Telegraph* property section on a Saturday. They wrote a one page article about me and the book which led to a surge in requests.

The book itself gave me instant credibility; I put it on my biography, I was seen as a serious business owner, and I was aligning myself with other successful people.

My goal with the book was solely to generate leads. I gave it away and still give it away. Not only has it helped me to create a larger property portfolio, owners have become better informed, and we have more educated discussions with less hard sell. For our owners, it has enabled them to increase bookings outside of the peak holiday season, give our families what they are looking for, so it's win-win for all of us.

Wendy Shand
www.totstotravel.com

Another way in which you can generate leads, which you may have noticed that I've done in this book, is to take readers outside of your book for additional resources that add value and encourage your readers to join your list.

There are various ways in which you can do this. You can see that I've included additional blueprints, downloads and checklists that you can access by leaving your name and email address on a specific page on my website. This means that I can build a relationship with you, share additional valuable information and find out how I can help further. It also allows you to develop these resources without needing to create a new edition of your book, as your content may change later or you may add extra bonuses.

Create products from your book

I've already alluded to the fact that you can use your book in many more ways. These include creating multiple streams of income from your knowledge, giving people the chance to access this in many different ways, so let me give you a few examples.

When I started writing this book, I launched a programme of the same name, which I mentioned earlier. I carried out three free webinars (the Summer Book-Camp) where I softly up-sold to the six week programme. This not only allowed me to write this book quickly – well it forced me to, actually! – it allowed me to make a bigger difference than I could just through the text in this book. By working through a series of live training sessions online, I was able to help the participants to take action, ask questions and make their book happen. Although a book like this will help you, there is something about working on a physical level with a person or group like this that helps them to actually take action. It is also available as a product through my website.

This is a process that I've followed for this book and my second, so please contact me to find out how I can help you to model this too, because it works!

What else could you do to create information products from your book?

- How about creating a workbook that your readers could work through?

- Perhaps you could create an audio or video series that would help them to take their learning to the next level?

- You could create an information product that you promote through your book, giving your readers a brilliant next step.

- You could also use your expertise to create a membership club. This is what I did after running my '90 Days to Stand out in your Business' programme in 2013. This became the foundation for The Business Wow Factor membership along with other short programmes, interviews and resources – www.thebusinesswowfactor.com.

- You can create a new online programme, and

this content becomes book two! You could upsell to this programme in your first book.

- You could run an event or workshop that supports the content in your book. This would be another good step as you'll get to meet some of your readers, and help them to use the information personally.

- Of course, working with clients one-to-one and taking them through your process on a personal level is a brilliant way to grow your business too.

- What other ways could you repackage, repurpose or extend your knowledge?

During the online programme, I was asked by one of the participants how to do this, and I believe that giving people different ways to access your knowledge is essential. You may find that reading this book will spur you to action and you don't need my support in any other way. Or you may want me to hold your hand each step of the way, give you more encouragement, and share even more of my secrets. When I work one-to-one with my clients, they get a bespoke service and I am there to motivate them and support them on an individual basis. If you'd like help in this area, please email me today at karen@selfdiscoverycoaching.co.uk as I'd love to have a chat and find out how I can help you.

Get business from speaking engagements

I'm not going to go into this in huge detail here

as I mentioned this extensively in the last section. However, I'd like to reiterate how writing a book has helped me to get some brilliant speaking engagements. Then the speaking engagements have allowed me to reach new clients and connect with people that I'd never have reached before being a published author.

Top tip: To get speaking opportunities, simply ask for them. Put a post on Facebook, share it on LinkedIn or write a tweet. Simply making the decision to speak will give you a platform to share your knowledge.

I've been invited to speak at many business and coaching groups since writing my books. Part of this has been personal choice, and I've also had phone calls asking me to present at events too. There has been one particular group that I have spoken at three times to date. To get to this venue involves a 220 mile round trip around the M25 and I'm not paid for the event. However, these three appearances have resulted in attracting five new one-to-one clients to date and numerous people who have joined one of my online programmes, attended my events, or bought my books. Of course, the best part of this is that I've been able to share my knowledge and expertise to make it easy for them!

Other ways to reach more people

Ultimately with your book and being a published author, you can reach more people than you can do with a website, blog and social media presence.

And surely that's why you came into business in the first place. As a coach, consultant, therapist or trainer this may have been your first motivation – I know it was mine. But as you have developed your business, you've quickly learnt that you do need to build a sustainable business (and income) to continue to help people. So what else can you do with your book to reach more people and make a bigger impact in the world?

What you now have is a sales tool in your hand. Something that you can promote that allows you to attract more clients who want to work with you, without feeling like you're selling to them. You have a tool that allows you to attract more publicity. It's easier for people to get what you do and how you can help them. Your book is the hook, so go ahead and use it!

Please keep in touch and I'd love to know the results that you've received from writing your book and getting noticed.

You can email me at
karen@selfdiscoverycoaching.co.uk,
call 023 9200 6418, or join my community at
www.selfdiscoverycoaching.co.uk.
I look forward to hearing from you.

About Karen Williams

- Karen Williams is a business coach and mentor who specialises in working with coaches, therapists and transformation experts. Her passion is helping them to get more clients, make more money and do what they love, specifically focusing on helping them to get noticed through writing a book.

- She is a qualified coach, NLP Master Practitioner and Firewalk Instructor. She is a speaker and the author of four business books and has contributed to four other books to date.

- Karen also loves to speak and do crazy stuff too, like jumping out of planes and helping people to walk on hot coals!

A dream to change the world

When Karen Williams trained as a coach, she wanted to change the world and soon realised that she could only do so one person at a time. Her passion is working with solopreneurs who want to make a difference. But they also know that to do this, they need to learn the skills to create and grow a successful business, and then have the courage to implement these.

She is known for helping her clients to succeed by standing out from the crowd, getting noticed and being an expert in their business – as well as overcoming the fear that might stop them. Through this she can create a ripple effect, as she gives them the resources, abilities and confidence to transform the lives of their clients and make a bigger difference.

Karen's journey

Karen's journey into business started in January 2006, when, after spending 15 years in the corporate world in human resources and training roles, she realised that she didn't want to do it anymore. She'd heard of this thing called coaching, and employed her first coach to get her career back on track. Not only did she find a new job, but she discovered a vocation that she really wanted to pursue. She trained as a coach and, in November 2006, Self Discovery Coaching was born.

But she thought it would be easy. She thought she could get 1,000 glossy brochures printed, order some business cards and set up a website. She thought she could go along to networking events and people would be clamouring for her services, but it didn't happen that way.

She became a career coach supporting people to find a job they love, but she knew that to be successful herself she needed to do more than just be a great coach. That's why she interviewed and learnt the secrets from more than 25 top performance coaches including Michael Neill, Dawn Breslin and Gladeana McMahon and published her first book based on what she'd learnt in 2011.

This first book was *The Secrets of Successful Coaches*, which became an Amazon bestseller, and her second book, *How to Stand Out in your Business*, was published in 2012, which shares her unique Seven Step Success System. Since 2010, she has been working with coaches, consultants and therapists in business to teach this learning and help her clients to get great business results.

Karen's passion is to help more people to write a book and in 2014 she ran her first writing retreat in Spain (www.writingretreats.co.uk) and wrote her third and fourth books. She is a speaker on inspiration, mindset, business and writing, and runs an annual conference – where she always does something a little bit different! She founded her online membership programme in November 2013, which is a community and business learning portal for coaches, therapists and solopreneurs.

She has also been featured on local TV, UK and international radio, in various publications including

Psychologies, *Marie Claire*, *Coaching at Work*, *Rapport* magazine, *Personnel Today*, the *Daily Express*, and *Portsmouth News*, and she speaks at events across the UK and abroad.

On a personal note

Karen has also conquered her own challenges. In her book *The Mouse that Roared* she shares some of these stories. This includes the 'Year to Live' project where in 2012 she decided to do things that she had never done before. Although happy with her life, she knew that there were things that she'd love to do.

During that year she decided to go skiing for the first time – after always saying she'd go one day. She also jumped out of a plane for charity (and took three of her clients and husband with her!). She also qualified as a Firewalk Instructor and has helped dozens of her clients to walk on hot coals, break through boards and walk across a bed of broken glass. But don't let that put you off!

In addition, she signed up to do a charity trek, and in September 2013 she walked the Inca Trail in Peru to Machu Picchu for the Genesis Research Trust (Women for Women) and was part of a group of 21 ladies who raised over £90,000 for charity. This was a bigger achievement than Karen had imagined as she was hospitalised in Peru just before the trek started, so she was glad to make it! Their fundraising was celebrated at the House of Lords in May 2014 with a presentation by Professor Lord Robert Winston.

Karen knows that through her work, teaching and writing she can support more people, and leave a legacy that will help future generations. And she wants to help you to do the same!

Contact Karen

Find out more about Karen and her work at www.selfdiscoverycoaching.co.uk and you can email karen@selfdiscoverycoaching.co.uk.

You can also follow Karen on Facebook at www.facebook.com/selfdiscoverycoaching and Twitter at @selfdiscovery.